KINDER GARDENS

*Growing minds through
children's gardens*

Written by Jean Warren, Sarah Ness,
and Brenda Mann Harrison

Illustrated by Barb Tourtillotte

Totline® Publications
A Division of Frank Schaffer Publications, Inc.
Torrance, California

Managing Editor: Mina McMullin
Editor: Kathleen Cubley
Copyeditor: Kathy Zaun
Editorial Assistant: Mary Newmaster
Graphic Designer (Inside): Jill Kaufman
Graphic Designer (Cover): Brenda Mann Harrison
Illustrator (Cover): Barb Tourtillotte
Production Manager: Janie Schmidt

ISBN: 1-57029-289-2

Printed in the United States of America
Published by Totline® Publications
23740 Hawthorne Blvd.
Torrance, CA 90505

Contents

Introduction

What better way to intrigue young minds than to get out of the classroom and dig in the dirt? Nature awaits adults and children alike with her bounty and her miracles. So take a break from the ordinary and plan your next theme unit using the many wonderful gardens for children found in this book.

Kinder Gardens presents twenty child-related garden ideas. Each garden unit is divided into two sections. In the first section, there are two pages filled with step-by-step directions showing you just how to set up your garden, plus general gardening advice and lots of helpful tips. The second section contains two pages filled with activities, songs, and games for extended learning fun across the curriculum.

Your children will have a wonderful time creating Pizza Gardens, Bird Sanctuaries, and so much more as they pull together to solve problems, estimate results, figure quantities, chart materials, divide chores, and plan ways to share the experience with others. Try planting one garden with your group, or break your class up into smaller groups, each responsible for a different garden.

For best results, we suggest you always check with a local garden store or cooperative extension to find out the best conditions for the garden you are planning in your particular area.

Happy gardening!

Gardening Basics

Basic Gardening Tools

Every gardener needs appropriate gardening tools. You can collect your gardening supplies by visiting thrift stores, asking parents to donate old (but still usable) tools, and even making some of your own. Having more than one of each tool will help when multiple children want to work in a garden. The list below includes many of the things you will need to plant and tend the gardens in this book.

- small shovel
- hand rake
- garden trowel
- dibble (for poking holes in soil)
- gardener's line (see directions below)
- spade
- hoe
- rake
- large pruning shears
- small pruning shears
- watering can
- basket (for collecting cuttings and weeds)
- appropriate clothing (boots, hat, apron, gloves, old pants, old shirt)

Gardener's Line

A gardener's line will help you plan out straight rows in which to plant seeds or starts. To make this helpful tool, gather two sturdy garden stakes and some heavy twine. Securely tie one end of the twine to one of the stakes and wrap the remaining twine around the other stake. To use the line, place the stake with the twine tied to it in the soil. Begin walking in the direction you want your row to go in, unwinding the twine off of the other stake as you go. When your row is the desired length, place the remaining stake in the ground and tie the other end of the twine to it. Use a spade to mark the row along the length of the line. Now you have a perfectly straight row in which to plant your seeds or starts.

Preparing Soil

Proper soil preparation can make all the difference in the beauty of your garden—it's also surprisingly simple to do. Your children will love helping with this down and dirty activity. You will need gardening tools such as hoes, rakes, and trowels. Purchase enough organic fertilizer to mix into the plot of soil you have set aside for your garden. First, clean your area by pulling all of the weeds and unwanted grasses. Children will love to help weed. Then till or rake all of the soil to loosen it. Spread the organic fertilizer evenly over the soil, and let your children use their gardening tools (and their hands) to help work the organic matter into the soil. Your soil is now ready for planting.

Selecting Plants

Nurseries, garden centers, and even supermarkets offer a dizzying array of plants to choose from. Sometimes, looks can be deceiving. When selecting plants, be sure to keep these simple guidelines in mind.

1. It's better to choose flowering plants that haven't yet bloomed, even though it's tempting to choose those in bloom. Plants that are already blooming may not have as much time to flower in your garden as those that haven't yet bloomed.

2. Select plants with strong stems, not those that are leaning, and especially not stems that are droopy or wilting.

3. It is important to check that the roots aren't dried out or packed too tightly in the container. To check the roots, turn the container sideways and ease the plant out far enough to inspect the roots.

Safety in the Garden

Before beginning any gardening project with your children, be sure to go over some safety rules and discuss them thoroughly with your children. The most important gardening rule is that no item used in the garden should be tasted or eaten. This includes seeds, plants, soil, and organic fertilizer. If you must use a chemical fertilizer, use it before the weekend, and select a brand that is pet-safe. Another thing to discuss with your children is the proper use of tools. Demonstrate how each tool should be used, and let the children practice with the tools before they do any gardening. They should be familiar with the tools before they use them in the garden.

Respecting the Garden

Talk with your children about how the plants in your garden will grow and change. Tell them that some plants are meant to be harvested, and some are meant to be enjoyed in the garden. To make this clear to your children, make some garden markers by covering squares of red construction paper with clear self-stick paper. Attach the red squares to garden stakes. Tell your children that plants with red markers beside them are meant to be enjoyed in the garden.

Another part of respecting the garden is not crushing the plants by walking on them or sitting on them. Let your children know which areas of the garden they can walk in and which areas to avoid. This is especially important before seeds have sprouted.

Tips for Gardening With Children

Weeding Children can become overly enthusiastic when weeding. To help your children distinguish between the plants they want and the weeds that they don't want in their garden, first find pictures of what your plants will look like. Cut them out and glue them to index cards. Then let your children take these cards to the garden when it is weeding time.

A Garden of Variety You already know that your children have short attention spans. A great way to capture and keep children's attention is to provide lots of task options and things that children can do immediately. Digging holes holds endless fascination, as does watering and weeding.

A Touch of Water Supervise children closely when they water the garden. Don't let them drown the plants they've worked so hard to grow. A good way to control watering is to fill watering cans with a set amount of water and have one child water in one section of the garden and one child water in another section of the garden. Let each of the children in your group water a section of the garden, and the job will be done correctly.

Digging in the Dirt Getting dirty is one of the main bonuses of gardening, especially for children. Supply appropriate clothing for your children and let them get the most out of the act of gardening without worrying about the mess.

Your Role To maximize the creativity, you will want to act as a role model and a facilitator rather than as a leader. Of course, safety concerns (see page 7) will require your immediate intervention, but after the purchase of the seeds or starts, planning and planting the garden should be the children's responsibility.

Sharing Supplies Many times you won't have enough tools to go around. A good way to avoid squabbles is to have several of each garden tool. You may also want to help children think of ways to share equally in the gardening chores. Ideas include assigning each child a row to tend, making a garden chore chart, or simply having each child work on a certain gardening task for a set amount of time before another child takes over.

Gardening Journal Throughout your garden project—from the planting and the growing to the care and harvesting—take photos of your children and their work. Use the photos in a bulletin board display when you invite parents to share and see the fruits of the harvest, or put the photographs in an album, and let the children take turns describing what is happening in each picture.

Gardening Resources

The activities in *Kinder Gardens* are sure to plant the seed of gardening interest in you and your children. Below are some resources for extending the garden learning and enjoyment.

ABC Book of Flowers for Young Gardeners, by Joann Stoker, Illus. by Gerald Stoker. Summerhouse Press, 1999. Reading level: All ages.

A Seed Grows: My First Look at a Plant's Life Cycle (Child's First Look at Nature—A Unique Flap-Book Series), by Pamela Hickman, Illus. by Heather Collins. Kids Can Press, 1997. Reading level: Ages four to eight.

Atlas of Plants (First Discovery Book), by Gallimard Jeunesse, Claude D. Delafosse, Sylvaine Perols. Cartwheel Books, 1996. Reading level: Ages four to eight.

The Children's Kitchen Garden: A Book of Gardening, Cooking, and Learning, by Georgeanne Brennan, Ethel Brennan, Marcel Barchechat, Ann Arnold. Ten Speed Press, 1997. Reading level: Ages four to eight.

A Child's Garden: Enchanting Outdoor Spaces for Children and Parents, by Molly Dannenmaier, Constance Herndon. Simon & Schuster, 1998. Reading level: All ages.

Eyewitness Explorers: Flowers, by David Burnie. DK Publishing, 1997. Reading level: Ages four to eight.

Faces in All Kinds of Places: A Worm's Eye View of Flowers, by Michael E. Ross. Yosemite Association, 1987. Reading level: Ages four to eight.

Flower, Why Do You Smell So Nice (I Want to Know), by Francesca Grazzini, Illus. by Chiara Carrer, Translated by Talia Wise. Kane/Miller Book Publishing, 1996. Reading level: Ages four to eight.

From Seed to Plant, Illus. by Gail Gibbons. Holiday House, 1993. Reading level: Ages four to eight.

Gardening With Children, by Beth Richardson, Photos by Lynn Karli. Taunton Press, 1988. Reading level: Ages three to five.

Green Thumbs: A Kid's Activity Guide to Indoor and Outdoor Gardening, by Laurie Carlson. Chicago Review Press, 1995. Reading level: Ages four to eight.

Hollyhock Days: Garden Adventures for the Young at Heart, by Sharon Lovejoy. Interweave Press, 1994. Reading level: All ages.

How a Seed Grows (Let's-Read-and-Find-Out Books), by Helene J. Jordan, Illus. by Loretta Krupinski. Harpercollins Juvenile Books, 1992. Reading level: All ages.

Kid's Gardening: A Kid's Guide to Messing Around in the Dirt, by Kevin Raftery, Kim Gilbert Raftery, Illus. by Jim M'Guinness. Klutz Press, 1989. Reading level: Ages four to eight.

Roots, Shoots, Buckets & Boots: Gardening Together With Children, by Sharon Lovejoy. Workman Publishing Company, 1999. Reading level: All ages.

Soup Garden

Summer soups are simply wonderful. You and your children can "grow" a summer soup with many different kinds of fresh vegetables—the more colorful the better!

You Will Need

SEEDS OR STARTS
any number of the following:
- potatoes (any variety)
- onions
- carrots
- cabbages
- peas (optional)
- broccoli (optional)
- green peppers (optional)
- zucchini (optional)

SUPPLIES
basic gardening tools

Soil and Location Fertile, well-drained soil in full sun. A loose, sandy loam or mulch will provide the best results for potatoes, onions, and carrots.

Space Allow room for the potatoes. If you are planting optional vegetables, be sure to allow plenty of space. Peas will need to be trellised (see directions on pea seed package).

Time Required This garden will take a couple of months to grow, as you will need to direct sow.

Planting the Garden Follow directions on seed packages for direct sowing, or carefully transplant starts (for your optional vegetables, such as peppers, broccoli, and zucchini). Be sure to plant nonenation-resistant peas before mid-March and enation-resistant varieties after the first of April (check seed packages for this information).

Potatoes should be planted 4 to 6 inches deep, 12 inches apart. For best results, plant prestarted onions 4 to 5 inches apart in a 1- to 1 ½-inch-deep trench. Plant the onions in a sunny area because the growth time will be shorter if they get more sun. To make it easier for little hands to plant tiny carrot seeds, mix the seeds with a little sand before sowing. Children can then spread handfuls of "seed sand" in shallow trenches. Because it will take several weeks for the carrot seeds to germinate, it is important to keep the seeded area evenly moist. Sow early cabbage types from March through June; later maturing types from May to early June.

Care With seeds, thin according to package directions when the seedlings reach the recommended height. Thin carrot seedlings several times. Weed and water as needed. Potatoes need watering on a regular basis. Cabbage plants thrive with good fertilization.

Harvesting Gently dig up a potato plant to see if the potatoes are the desired size. A garden fork works best to minimize crop damage. Carrots taste best when their color is a bright orange. Onions can be used in a soup at any time, but they are mature when their tops begin to dry out and are falling over. Cut cabbage heads from the stems, leaving two or three of the wrapper leaves to protect it. Over-mature heads usually split.

What Kids Can Do

Encourage your children to help with as many parts of this garden as possible! They can mark the rows, plant the seeds, water, and weed. They will especially enjoy helping you harvest, wash, and chop the vegetables for the soup.

Simple Soup

2 large potatoes, chopped

½ cup diced onion

2 medium carrots, chopped

½ head cabbage, chopped

3 cups chicken broth

1 cup milk

seasonings such as pepper, basil, savory, thyme, and crushed garlic

Saute chopped potatoes, onion, and carrots gently until onions become transparent. Add chicken broth and cabbage, and bring to a gentle boil. Reduce heat and simmer until vegetables are tender, about 20 minutes. Add milk and seasonings as desired. Serve warm.

The Dirt on Gardening
COMPOSTING

As your children make a summer soup from the vegetables in their garden, what will they do with the greens they chop off and the skins they peel? Learn about composting, of course!

Explain that compost is basically new, nutrient-rich soil made from old organic waste. Good compost needs both nitrogen and carbon. That's easy to remember: green things (such as grass and vegetable scraps) add nitrogen; brown materials (such as leaves and sawdust) add carbon.

You can make dark, crumbly, sweet-earth-smelling compost indoors in a flowerpot. Choose a medium-size clay pot (about 10 inches in diameter). In the bottom of the pot, place a heavy layer of sawdust, straw, or wood chips. This will ensure adequate drainage for the compost. Add a layer of finely chopped vegetable scraps and then a layer of any combination of grass clippings, leaves, crushed eggshells, or used coffee grounds. Keep layering your compost until the mixture is about two inches from the top of the pot. Water the compost until damp. Keep the compost moist, and have your children stir it with a stick several times a week. After one month, dump out the mixture and see how much it has decomposed. Return it to the pot and continue watering and stirring until the compost is dark and crumbly. Use the compost in your next garden!

Soup

The Soup Is Boiling Up
Sung to: "The Farmer in the Dell"

The soup is boiling up,
The soup is boiling up.
Stir slow, around we go,
The soup is boiling up.

First we make the broth,
First we make the broth.
Stir slow, around we go,
The soup is boiling up.

Now we add some carrots,
Now we add some carrots.
Stir slow, around we go,
The soup is boiling up.

Continue with similar verses, using other vegetable names. Have the children stand around a large imaginary pot and pretend to stir the soup as they sing.

Jean Warren

Stone Soup

Read or tell the folktale "Stone Soup." Be sure the children understand how the villagers were tricked. Then ask your children if they would like to make their own Stone Soup. Pour two quarts of water into a large pot and let the children put in a round, smooth stone that has been scrubbed and boiled. Let the children help you chop up vegetables from their garden, such as carrots, cabbage, potatoes, onions, and zucchini. Bring the soup to a boil and then let it simmer, covered, for about one hour. When the vegetables are tender, add instant broth or bouillon and season to taste.

The Vegetable Man Story

Let your children take turns filling in the words to this story.

While I was walking down the street
A vegetable man I happened to meet.
His head was a bumpy _____.
His arms were long _____.
His body was a large _____.
His legs were two green _____.
He looked so good that on a hunch,
I invited him home for a big soup lunch!

Jean Warren

Variation: Cut out felt vegetables and let your children create vegetable men on a flannelboard as you recite the story.

Soup Pot Art

Collect pictures of various soup vegetables from magazines and seed catalogs. Give each of your children a piece of construction paper cut into the shape of a soup pot. Let them select the vegetable pictures they want in their soup, tear them out, and paste them onto their soup pots.

Variation: Give your children alphabet-shaped pasta or macaroni to glue onto their soup pictures.

Vegetable Sorting

Set out freshly-picked vegetables from your garden along with sheets of construction paper in vegetable colors, such as red, yellow, green, and brown. Let your children take turns sorting the vegetables by placing them on the matching colored pieces of paper.

Salad Garden

Growing a Salad Garden is a great way to interest your children in gardening and healthy eating.

You Will Need

SEEDS OR STARTS
You will want seeds for everything except tomatoes and cucumbers unless started indoors.

- lettuce
- radishes
- chives
- green onions
- spinach
- peas
- nasturtium
- cherry tomatoes
- cucumbers

SUPPLIES
basic gardening tools

compost or aged manure

tomato cages

bamboo stakes

Soil and Location Your Salad Garden will need fertile, well-drained soil. Choose a spot that gets at least six hours of sun, especially if you plan to grow tomatoes and cucumbers.

Space A 5-foot-by-5-foot or larger space is needed. If you do not have that much ground to dedicate to your Salad Garden, you can always use containers. Cucumbers and peas can crawl up a trellis.

> ## What Kids Can Do
> Your children will enjoy making their own plant markers (see page 59 for more details) and harvesting the vegetables. With supervision, children can plant seeds, too.

Time Required Start harvesting baby lettuce leaves in about four weeks. Harvest radishes, chives, and green onions six to eight weeks after planting. Peas, nasturtiums, cherry tomatoes, and cucumbers will take eight to twelve weeks.

Planting the Garden Prepare the soil by weeding and clearing out rocks. Add compost and use a hoe to work it into the soil. Follow directions on seed packages for direct sowing or carefully transplant starts. Distribute the seeds as thinly as possible and cover with soil. Water well and keep the soil damp while seeds germinate. In late spring or early summer, harden off tomato and cucumber starts and plant outdoors. For bushy plants like tomatoes, which produce many heavy fruit, you can buy wire cages that surround the whole plant. Put a cage over each seedling, and it will grow inside the cage. The branches will poke through the bars, which will support them while they bear fruit. The cage also keeps the fruit off the ground where it could be damaged or eaten by bugs. Plant cucumber seeds in mounds. Once each cucumber seedling has six leaves, thin the mound to just four seedlings. Cucumbers grow on a vigorous bush with 2-inch, triangular leaves. Each blossom produces a cucumber. To identify your plants, place plant markers near each group of seeds or starts.

Care Lettuce, radishes, and spinach will need to be thinned. Remember that the little sprouts you thin out are edible, too! To keep peas and tomatoes growing tall, insert a stake into the ground next to the plant, and secure the plants to the stake with twine. You can also use tomato cages or trellises for the pea plants. When your tomato seedlings get to be about 1 foot tall, pinch out the growth that comes up between the main stalk and a lateral branch. Choose a cloudy day or late afternoon to plant your tomatoes. The seedlings are delicate and will get transplant shock and wilt in too much sun. When planting seedlings, remove the bottom leaves halfway up the main stem. This will help develop a larger root system. If you live in an area with snails or slugs, you can keep them away by sprinkling some powdered ginger around your plants. Or, you can try sprinkling crushed eggshells around the base of the plants. The slugs don't like to climb over the sharp edges, plus the shells provide nutrients for the soil.

Tip
If you have pets or if wild animals have access to your garden area, you might want to look for a protected area such as a raised bed, or provide short fencing.

Harvesting For the best flavor, harvest lettuce and spinach early or late in the day. You can harvest leaves from lettuce plants as soon as they are large enough to snip off with scissors. This process is called "cut and come again." Make sure you don't wait too long to harvest radishes, or they get very spicy and tough and will go to seed. Feel around the base of the radishes to see if they are large enough to eat, and then pull them gently out of the ground. Pick tomatoes when they are perfectly red—they will be the best-flavored tomatoes you have ever tasted. Your tomatoes will ripen from late summer through the fall. In September, listen to the weather reports for frost warnings. Once frost hits the plants, the fruit will turn black, and you can pull up the plants and compost them. Pick peas when their pods are nice and plump. Regular harvesting promotes the formation of more pods. Cut the pea pods down the middle to expose the peas, then scoop them out. Cut chives any time all summer long. Pull green onions out of the ground when they are about 8 to 12 inches long. Don't allow cucumbers to get overripe or the vines will stop producing more cucumbers. Nasturtium flowers can be picked at any time for a delightful garnish.

The Dirt on Gardening

SLUG TRAPS

You can make an inexpensive slug trap from a few household items. Gather a plastic soda bottle (any size will do), dry cat food, and some tape. Cut the top off the bottle at the point where the straight part starts to taper. Invert the top back into the bottle and tape around the edges. Drop a few pieces of cat food inside the trap and set it on its side outdoors, wherever you've noticed slug damage. In a few days, you should find slugs inside. Throw out the whole trap and start over with a new one, or remove the slugs, replace the cat food, and place the trap back in the "sluggy" area.

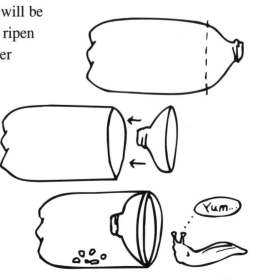

Yum...

Salad

Salad Bar

Let your children help you set up a Salad Bar. With supervision, let each child help scrub, slice, or grate various salad vegetables. At snacktime, set out the ingredients with serving spoons and let your children create their own salads. You might even want to turn this into a salad party by inviting another school group or parents to join you.

Totally Green Salad

Let your children help you decide what they might put into a totally green salad. Let them choose from such vegetables as lettuce, cucumbers, zucchini, green onions, and green peppers. This snack is especially fun for St. Patrick's Day.

Designer Dressing

Just as with salads, children love being inventive by creating their own salad dressing. Set out such ingredients as cottage cheese, mayonnaise, milk, various herbs, or some vegetable soup mix. Let your children measure out 1 to 1½ cups of the cottage cheese or mayonnaise and enough milk to make the dressing appropriately thin, and place it all in a blender. Let them decide which spices to add. Blend and place in a bowl. Let the children drizzle a spoonful onto their salads.

Patterning With Vegetable Rounds

When working with vegetables, take the opportunity to show your children how to recognize and repeat patterns. On a tray, set out a pattern of vegetable rounds, such as carrot-zucchini-carrot-zucchini. Give each child a sheet of waxed paper, a pile of carrot rounds, and a pile of zucchini rounds. Have them repeat your pattern on their pieces of waxed paper. Then let them dip the veggie rounds in some dip and enjoy eating them.

French Dressing

Have children combine the following ingredients into a jar: three-fourths cup of vegetable oil, four tablespoons lemon juice, one teaspoon Worcestershire sauce, two teaspoons ketchup, one teaspoon paprika, one teaspoon honey, and one teaspoon salt. Tightly seal the jar and let your children take turns shaking it to mix the dressing.

Salad Art

Give each of your children some shredded lettuce, some carrot rounds, a couple of cherry tomatoes, and some cucumber slices. Encourage your children to arrange their vegetables on a paper plate in an interesting design. Let the children share their designs with each other before they sit down to gobble up their artwork.

Pizza Garden

Your children will love pizza even more when they plant, grow, and harvest their own ingredients.

You Will Need

SEEDS OR STARTS

Starts are recommended. Choose the specific varieties you would like, considering the following recommendations:

- tomato (almost any variety but cherry)
- basil (sweet Italian would be best)
- onions (any sweet variety)
- oregano
- thyme (garden or winter)

SUPPLIES

basic gardening tools

Soil and Location Fertile, well-drained soil in full sun.

Space Allow enough room for each tomato plant to bush out a couple of feet.

Time Required Using starts will speed the harvest time. Depending on the maturity of your starts, allow one to two months for tomatoes and onions to mature. Allow an additional month if you direct sow.

Planting the Garden In well-prepared soil, mark the space needed for each kind of plant or seeds. Plan to put the larger-maturing tomato plants in the back row, followed by basil and oregano, with onions and thyme in the front. Directly sow seeds according to package directions or carefully transplant the starts, gently massaging the roots and pressing around the stems when planted. Water seeds with a light but thorough sprinkling of water. Water at the base of transplanted starts.

Care With seeds, thin according to package directions as the seedlings reach the recommended height. For both seeds and starts, weed and water as needed. Support growing tomato bushes with a trellis or tomato cage.

Harvesting Depending on variety, most onions are ready when they appear to have a good bulb below the surface. Gently pluck ripe tomatoes off the vine. Use scissors to trim the desired amount of herbs off the ends of the plants. For basil, cut the top leaves and stems, leaving at least six inches of the plant remaining.

Extra Fun

For added fun, make your Pizza Garden in the shape of a pizza pie, with a wedge for each kind of plant. Consider using a Hula-Hoop to mark the edge of your circular garden. Tie five 2-foot-long strings to a garden stake and anchor it in the middle of your circle. Fan out the strings to the edge of the Hula-Hoop to define the edges of the wedges. Secure the ends of the strings to craft sticks or garden stakes. Plant one type of seed or start in each "slice."

Did You Know?

- Tomatoes and basil taste great together, and they are a natural combination in a growing garden. Each plant releases nutrients into the soil that the other plant needs. This type of relationship is good for healthy gardens. So put your companion plants together as often as you can!

- Maturing tomato plants do best if the leaves do not get wet when watered. Water the plant at the soil level only, not from above, and use warm water if possible. Cold water shocks the roots and slows down growth.

What Kids Can Do

Your children can help mark the rows, plant the seeds and starts, water, and weed. They will especially enjoy harvesting. Basil, oregano, and thyme can easily be cut with good-quality, child-safe scissors. Have the children put their cut herbs and produce into a basket or plastic bowl—not metal—for easier carrying.

The Dirt on Gardening

SOIL PREPARATION

Seeds germinate better and plants grow and thrive in a healthy environment. A healthy environment begins with well-prepared soil.

First locate a site that will suit the needs of your plants. Using a garden fork or spade, dig up the sod. Scrape off as much excess soil as you can and remove the remaining sod chunks.

Once the sod is removed, till your soil by digging deep and turning the earth over with each scoop. Break up the chunks of earth using a hoe. Have your children help rake everything smooth, removing undesirable root balls and rocks.

Use your hands or a hoe to work in compost and a good organic fertilizer and then rake smooth again.

Tip

Save the rocks or pebbles you find in your garden space for your Rock Garden (see pages 86 and 87), your Indoor Garden (pages 74 and 75), or your Cup Terrarium (pages 66 and 67).

Pizza

English Muffin Pizzas

Split English muffins (one muffin half for each of your children) and toast them under a broiler. Set out the toasted muffin halves, some pizza sauce (see recipe below), and bowls of mozzarella cheese, pineapple chunks, sliced olives, chopped green peppers, and other pizza toppings. Let your children use spoons to spread the sauce onto their muffin halves. Next, have them place other desired ingredients on their muffins, topping them off with cheese. Place the children's pizzas on a foil-lined baking sheet, writing each child's name on the foil near his or her pizza. Broil until the cheese is hot and bubbly. Allow pizzas to cool before serving.

Making Pizza Sauce

Let your children make their own pizza sauce from the ingredients found in their Pizza Garden. Have them pick four or five tomatoes and wash them. Help your children chop the tomatoes into small pieces. Add the chopped tomatoes to a can of tomato sauce combined with two tablespoons of tomato paste. Let the children stir in spices such as oregano, basil, thyme, parsley, garlic powder, and salt. Simmer over low heat (or microwave) until warm and then spread on English muffin halves and top with cheese and pizza veggies.

Pizza Art

For each child, cut a large yellow or light brown "pizza crust" and the following "toppings" out of construction paper: small red circles for tomatoes, brown circles for sausages, white spirals for onions, black ovals for olives, green squares for peppers, and white mushroom shapes for mushrooms. Then give the children their pizzas and let them glue on their choice of toppings.

Pizza Flip

Try this fun coordination game with your children. Let your children take turns flipping a large cardboard pizza. Decorate a large cardboard cake round to resemble a pizza. Place the pizza on a round aluminum pizza pan. Have your children hold onto the sides of the pizza pan and flip the cardboard pizza up and over. Then have them flip it back again. Continue while interest lasts, letting each child have a turn.

I Wish I Were a Pepperoni Pizza

Sung to: "The Oscar Meyer Theme Song"

Oh, I wish I were a pepperoni pizza,
That is what I'd really like to be.
For if I were a pepperoni pizza,
Everyone would be in love with me!

Let your children take turns naming their favorite kinds of pizza and singing about them.

Jean Warren

I Like Pizza

Sung to: "Skip to My Lou"

I like pizza, yes, I do.
I like pizza, yes, I do.
I like pizza, yes, I do.
And my tummy likes it, too!

Naomi Lurey and Sharon Moscicki

Harvest Garden

Some pleasures are slow to develop, but the rewards are bountiful. Your children will discover that a Harvest Garden is worth the wait. The fun begins in the spring and fulfills itself in early autumn with a harvest of good things to enjoy.

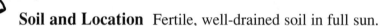

Soil and Location Fertile, well-drained soil in full sun.

Space This kind of garden loves to spread out! You can choose to have one or two plants of each kind or an entire plot of land. Whatever space you choose, make sure the site can stay undisturbed until early autumn.

Time Required Depending on your specific varieties, anticipate approximately 70 to 120 days for maturity.

Planting the Garden Follow directions on seed packages. Plant the highest number of recommended seeds to ensure germination—you can always thin later.

- Because it is wind pollinated, corn does best if planted in blocks of at least four rows. If you plant both sweet and ornamental corn, it is best to separate them.

- Pumpkins need many visits by bees to produce good fruit. If your Harvest Garden is not near pollen-bearing flowers, you might want to consider adding bee-attracting plants to the area.

Care Thin seedlings according to package directions, leaving the strongest plants. Your Harvest Garden will benefit from several feedings of complete organic fertilizers. Pumpkins do best with regular watering. Sunflowers, however, need thorough but infrequent watering to promote deep roots and strong stems.

You Will Need

SEEDS
any number of the following:

- corn (sweet corn or ornamental corn, or both)
- gourds
- mini pumpkins
- carving pumpkins
- sunflowers (giant variety as well as smaller kinds for cutting)

SUPPLIES
basic gardening tools

Harvesting When the silk on sweet corn ears appears dry or brown, the sweet corn is ready to be picked and eaten. You want the kernels to be full and milky. Ornamental corn should be left on the stalk until the husks begin to dry. Sunflowers do best when picked early in the morning. Gourds and pumpkins are ready to be picked when their rinds have turned hard.

What Kids Can Do

Your children can help with many parts of this garden! They can help mark the rows, plant the seeds (which are a good size for small hands), water, and weed. They will especially enjoy harvesting. An adult should cut the pumpkins and gourds off the vines.

Gourd Fun

Turn a gourd into a birdhouse. Bottleneck gourd seeds produce a large gourd with a long, narrow neck and a wide base, up to 10 inches. When their skins turn brown, harvest the gourds and let them dry in a protected place. Hollow them out and use them as unique birdhouses.

The Dirt on Gardening

EARTH'S CYCLE

Gardening lets children experience firsthand the life cycle of earth's plants. Feeling the dirt, raking it smooth, planting seeds, watering, watching, weeding, then waiting and harvesting all give children an appreciation for our Earth.

This appreciation can extend beyond the growing process. To help children understand that growth leads to death, decay, and new growth again, let all or part of your Harvest Garden stand over the winter—after you have removed all usable fruits and vegetables.

Watch the plants become a source of food and shelter for wildlife, slowly droop and decay, and all the while adding nutrients to the soil.

Sunflowers are the ideal plant to leave standing in the garden for birds to use as food. What happens to the stalks throughout the winter? What do they look like in early spring? Encourage your children to look at the ground around the old sunflowers to see if any dropped seeds bring new surprises in the spring. You might even see "volunteer" sunflowers after you till!

Fall

Pumpkin Printing

After Halloween, use your carved jack-o'-lantern for printmaking. Cut the pumpkin into chunks, and let your children use large nails to carve designs on the insides of the pumpkin pieces. Then have them press the design sides of their pumpkin pieces on ink pads and then on pieces of construction paper.

Jack-o'-Lantern Matching

Make six pairs of pumpkin faces on twelve white index cards. Let your children take turns matching the pumpkin faces. If desired, start with only four cards (two pairs) and increase the number of pairs as the children's abilities increase.

Sequence Cards

On four large index cards, draw the growth stages of a pumpkin (a seed, a flowering vine, a green pumpkin, and a ripe pumpkin). Mix up the cards and let the children take turns putting them in order.

Extension: Make sequence cards showing the growth cycle of other fall vegetables.

Counting Pumpkin Seeds

Before you clean out a pumpkin to turn it into a jack-o'-lantern, have your children guess how many seeds they will find inside. Write down their guesses. Have your class clean out the pumpkin, preserving the seeds in a special pan. Later, after you have washed the seeds and before you cook them for a snack, let your group help you count them. Which child guessed the closest?

Corncob Prints

Wash corncobs and let them dry for several days. Make paint pads by placing folded paper towels in shallow containers and pouring on liquid tempera paint. To make prints, let the children roll the corncobs on the paint pads, then roll the cobs across sheets of construction paper.

Lanterns

When carving pumpkins to make jack-o'-lanterns, don't forget that other vegetables, such as squash and gourds, were also used as lanterns many years ago.

Time for Corn

Read the poem below and let your children act out the movements.

Great big giant cornstalk,
Growing in the sun.
Ripe, juicy ears of corn—
Let's pick some.

Juicy tender yellow corn,
Put it in the pot.
Pour in the water,
Cook it till it's hot.

Juicy, sweet, tender corn,
Ready on the plate.
Is it time for dinner?
I can't wait!

Jean Warren

Butterfly Garden

Your children will love the rewards of creating this garden—butterflies to observe and enjoy!

You Will Need

PLANT LIST

Nectar sources for adult butterflies: abelia (*Abelia x grandiflora*), aster (*Aster novae-angliae*), black-eyed Susan (*Rudbeckia hirta*), blanket flower (*Gaillardia*), butterfly bush (*Buddleia davidii*), coreopsis (*Coreopsis*), daylily (*Hemerocallis*), milkweed (*Asclepias*), phlox (*Phlox paniculata*), purple coneflower (*Echinacea purpurea*), sunflower (*Helianthus*), sweet alyssum (*Lobularia maritima*), verbena (*Verbena bonariensis*), yarrow (*Achillea millefolium*)

Butterfly host plants: Monarch Queen butterfly—various native milkweed (*Asclepieas*); Viceroy butterfly—various willow (*Salix*); Mourning Cloak butterfly—various aspen (*Populus*); Cloudless Sulphur butterfly—partridge pea (*Chamaecrista fasciculata*); Sleepy Orange butterfly—coffee senna (*Senna occidentails*), Maryland senna (*Cassia marilandica*); Buckeye butterfly—false foxglove (*Agalinus*), toadflax (*Linaria*), Indian paintbrush (*Castilleja*); Great Spangled Fritillary, Aphrodite Fritillary, and Atlantis Fritillary butterflies—various violets (*Viola*); Spring Azure Celastrina Ladon butterfly—flowers of many plants including dogwoods (*Cornus*), viburnums (*Viburnum*), buckeye (*Aesculus*), sumac (*Rhus*), black snakeroot (*Cimicifuga racemeosa*); Red Admiral butterfly—common nettle (*Urtica dioica*), pellitory (*Parietaria*); American Painted Lady butterfly—pearly everlasting (*Anaphalis margaritacea*), sweet everlasting (*Psudognaphalium obtusifolium*)

Larva host plants: butterfly bush (*Buddleia davidii*), camphor tree (*Cinnamomum camphora*), various native milkweed (*Asclepieas*), sassafras (*Sassafras albidum*), spicebush (*Lindera benzion*), white clover (*Trifolium repens*)

SUPPLIES

basic gardening tools

Soil and Location Your Butterfly Garden will need at least six hours of full sun per day and average, well-drained soil.

Space You can turn an existing part of your garden into a butterfly haven. If you already have some host plants, just add to them. Or, plant the garden outside a window in your room. This way, you and your children can enjoy watching the butterflies even when you're indoors.

Time Required Once you provide the habitat and water the butterflies need, you should start to notice them in the summer.

Planting the Garden You will want to choose plants from each category—host plants for butterflies, nectar plants for adult butterflies, and host plants for the larvae. First, identify which plants you already have and then select additional plants from the lists provided. Butterflies lay their eggs on plants that produce food for the caterpillars and that provide shelter and camouflage for the cocoons. Choose an area close to a colorful wall or other surface. Butterflies are attracted to large blocks of color. Group together plants with similar needs (soil, light, and exposure). Other items that will help attract butterflies include dark, flat stones and a water source. Butterflies can bask in the sun on the stones, dry their wings, and warm their bodies for flying. Make sure there are shallow water puddles for your butterflies. The males of many species will congregate in "drinking clubs," most likely to obtain the salts and amino acids they need.

Care Keep new plants watered the first year. In addition, you will want to deadhead spent flowers and divide perennials when necessary. Perennials will need to be divided every few years, and be fertilized or composted once a year. Avoid using pesticides, even organic ones, or you will destroy your intended guests.

Did You Know?

Most adult butterflies only live two or three weeks. In that brief period of time, they must find a mate, reproduce, find food and shelter, and avoid being eaten.

The Dirt on Gardening

PLANTING SEEDS

When seeds are very tiny or if their color makes them difficult to see against the soil, you can use one of the methods described below to make seed planting easier.

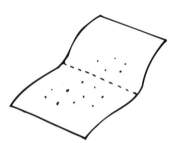

Toilet Paper Method
Make a shallow trench in your garden in the row where you want to plant your tiny seeds. Lay a strip of toilet paper in the trench and drop your seeds onto the paper. Gently sprinkle the soil on top of the seeds.

Gently but thoroughly water the row, and your seeds will start to grow as the toilet paper rots away. Single ply and recycled toilet papers are cheaper and better for the seeds because they do not contain dyes or bleaches, and they break down more quickly.

Seed Tape Method Stick tiny seeds to the sticky side of a strip of masking tape. Place the tape seed-side up in a shallow trench in the garden and cover it with the correct amount of soil. The tape will disintegrate as your seeds grow.

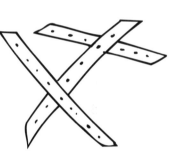

Seed Goop Method Mix one cup of cornstarch and one cup of cold water in a saucepan. Stir well to dissolve any lumps. Carefully bring the mixture to a simmer. Continue to simmer until thick and syruplike. Let the mixture cool to the point where you can touch it without burning yourself. Gently stir in your seeds. Pour the "goop" into a resealable plastic bag and seal the bag. Prepare a shallow trench in the garden where you want the seeds to grow. Snip off a corner of the bag and squeeze the goop into the trench. Cover the goop with the correct amount of soil and wait for your seeds to sprout.

Butterflies

Butterfly Dance

Use safety pins or strong tape to attach colorful crepe-paper butterfly wings to your children's clothes. Play some music and have the children pretend to be butterflies and flutter around the room. Stop the music and have them freeze in place. Then start the music again.

Extension: Videotape the Butterfly Dance. The streamers sail gracefully through the air, and the whole scene is lovely to watch. Your children will want to watch their Butterfly Dance over and over again.

Clothespin Butterflies

Cover a table with newspaper and set out pieces of white tissue paper. Mix different colors of food coloring with water and put the separate colors into spray bottles. Have the children carefully spray the colored water on the tissue paper. Allow the water to dry. Cut the tissue paper into 4-by-6-inch rectangles. Give each child two tissue-paper rectangles and a wooden slot-type clothespin. Have the children insert their tissue paper pieces into the slots of their clothespins as shown to make butterflies. Place the butterflies all around the room.

Variation: Glue magnetic strips to the backs of the clothespins to make butterfly magnets.

The Miracle of Butterflies

Catch a caterpillar this spring, or order one from a science supply catalog. Let your children help you fill a Mason jar with some "homey" things such as a twig and bits of grass. Use a hammer and a nail to poke small holes in the jar lid. Put the caterpillar in the jar and screw on the lid. Let your children enjoy watching the caterpillar spin a cocoon and evolve into a butterfly or moth. Open the jar outdoors, and watch the butterfly flutter away.

Hint: Butterfly larvae and holding pens are available from the Delta School Supply catalog, P.O. Box 3000, Nashua, NH 03061-3000, or call 800-442-5444 to order.

Butterfly, Butterfly

Sung to: "Jingle Bells"

Butterfly, butterfly,
Dancing all around.
Butterfly, butterfly,
Now you're on the ground.
In a tree, hard to see,
Now you've flown away.
Butterfly, oh butterfly,
Please come back some day.

Gee Gee Drysdale

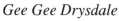

Colorful Butterflies

Cut large butterfly shapes out of construction paper and wallpaper samples. Hang the shapes from the ceiling. Talk about the colorful butterflies when introducing colors and patterns.

Variation: Cover several of the butterfly shapes with clear self-stick paper, and cut each one into three or four puzzle pieces. Let the children put the butterfly puzzles together while talking about the colors.

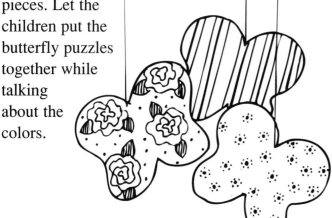

Color Flannelboard Poem

Cut out five butterflies, one each from the following colors of felt: red, blue, yellow, green, and white. Let your children help you add the appropriate butterfly to the flannelboard as you read the poem below. You may also want to add some felt flowers to your flannelboard.

The first little butterfly to the flower bed
Is a pretty little butterfly colored red.

Next comes a butterfly colored blue.
Such a pretty butterfly, now there are two.

Number three is a sunny fellow.
Number three has wings of yellow.

Next comes a butterfly, the best I've seen—
This beautiful butterfly is colored green.

Last comes a butterfly, a glorious sight—
This beautiful butterfly is colored white.

Adapted from a poem by Susan M. Paprocki

Ladybug Garden

With their bright colors against the green of growing leaves, ladybugs are the jewels of a garden. By eating bad bugs known to destroy healthy plants, ladybugs are also the champions of good deeds. Introduce your children to these gardeners' friends.

You Will Need

SUPPLIES

a clear-plastic or glass container and a cover punched with air holes

washed gravel

lump-free dirt

leafy starts, small plants, and other greens

water

nature items such as sticks and rocks

ladybugs

aphids

Ladybugs are a gardener's best bug friend. These bright, round beetles come in a variety of colors. They can be red, yellow, orange, gray, and black. They can be colored with or without spots. The most common ladybug has a red-orange back with a black head.

Gardeners like to have ladybugs stay in their gardens because they eat aphids. Aphids are tiny bugs that collect and multiply on plants, eating and destroying them.

Planting the Garden Your ladybug viewing center can be as elaborate or as simple as you would like. If you intend to keep the bugs for observation for a couple of days, try to make the ladybugs comfortable. Put a little washed gravel in the bottom of your clear-plastic or glass container. Add a layer of clump-free dirt or potting soil. Plant a few small lettuce starts or other garden plants. Even a small clump of grass will provide a green environment. Add a few ladybugs.

Put on the lid punched with air holes (make sure the holes are smaller than your bugs!) and watch your ladybugs. Be sure to keep the container away from bright light that might overheat the bugs. Now find a ladybug's favorite food—aphids. Some species of aphids are large; others are so small you need a magnifying glass to see them. Aphids suck the liquid out of plants, weakening leaves and stems. You will find them gathered on flower buds and on new growth on vegetable plants. Snip off an infected piece and add it to your ladybug jar. Remember to release your ladybugs after a couple of days.

Hint If you want to encourage ladybugs to hang around your garden, plant the plants they like. Ladybugs seem to be fond of tansy, angelica, scented geranium, leafy greens, and sweet corn.

Ladybug Young Ones

Although the mature ladybug is easily recognized, the young larvae are not. A young larva hatches from a yellow-orange egg, usually laid on the underside of a leaf, and immediately starts devouring aphids. One larva can eat from 30 to 40 aphids a day. Because of their voracious appetite, ladybug larvae are sometimes called "aphid lions." These larvae are about ½-inch long and look somewhat like a little alligator that is flattened and narrower at the head and tail ends. Just like the adult beetles, ladybug larvae can be all different colors.

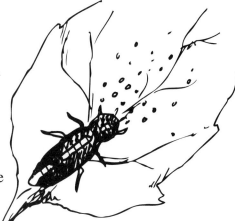

Did You Know?

- In Old English, the word *lady* first meant "the head farmer's wife." The term *ladybug* is associated with that meaning, as this bug is the most beneficial aid to a farmer or a gardener.

- In England, ladybugs are commonly called "Ladybird beetles," because of an English dislike for the word *bug*.

- In Germany, ladybugs are considered good luck. Replicas of ladybugs are used as Christmas tree decorations.

What Kids Can Do

Your children can help prepare the temporary ladybug home. They will enjoy searching for ladybugs to put into the viewing center, but encourage them to be gentle. Let all your children participate in the final release of the ladybugs.

The Dirt on Gardening

WHERE TO FIND LADYBUGS

You can purchase ladybug beetles from a variety of sources—commercial suppliers, farmers' co-ops, and some nurseries. Inquire early about the best time of year to buy ladybugs (usually summer).

Ladybugs introduced to a garden area have a reputation for flying off either right away or as soon as the food supply runs short. To encourage them to stay, try some of the following ideas:

- Dampen plants before releasing the beetles.

- Release the ladybugs just before sunrise or just after the sun sets.

- Don't just sprinkle the beetles about. Instead, gently lay handfuls of ladybugs at the base of aphid-infested plants where they'll find lunch right away.

Ladybugs

Ladybug Prints

Have your children make ladybug shapes by pressing their thumbs onto red stamp pads and then onto white paper. Then let them turn their thumbprints into ladybugs by adding dots and six legs to each one with black felt tip markers.

Ladybug Vests

Your children will love decorating and wearing their own ladybug costumes. To make a vest, cut a large paper grocery sack straight down the middle from top to bottom, as shown in the illustration. Cut a neck hole in the bottom and armholes in the sides. Have your children use black markers to add dots to their vests, and away they fly!

Observing Ladybugs

Ladybugs (also know as ladybird beetles) are friends to gardeners everywhere. They eat aphids and insects that might otherwise harm plants. Introduce your children to these friendly creatures by catching them in your ladybug garden or by purchasing some from a garden supply store. Place them in a glass cage or other container. Encourage your children to observe the ladybugs. How many spots do they have? Do they all look the same? Your children may be surprised to learn that ladybugs aren't all ladies—some are male, and others are female. Their vivid coloring warns birds and other potential predators that they are not a tasty meal. When you and your children are finished with your ladybugs, release them back into your garden.

Ladybugs are available from the Delta School Supply catalog, P.O. Box 3000, Nashua, NH 03061-3000, or by calling 800-442-5444.

Ladybug, Ladybug, Fly Around

Cut out a set of four large, colored-paper leaves (red, green, yellow, and blue) for each of your children. Lay the leaves on the ground around each of your children. As you recite the poem below, have the children perform the actions described and "land" on the appropriate colored leaf.

Ladybug, ladybug, fly around.
Ladybug, ladybug, touch the ground.
Ladybug, ladybug, scratch your head.
Ladybug, ladybug, land on red.

Ladybug, ladybug, fly around.
Ladybug, ladybug, touch the ground.
Ladybug, ladybug, wiggle like Jell-O,
Ladybug, ladybug, land on yellow.

Ladybug, ladybug, fly around.
Ladybug, ladybug, touch the ground.
Ladybug, ladybug, shine your wings. (Rub arms.)
Ladybug, ladybug, land on green.

Ladybug, ladybug, fly around.
Ladybug, ladybug, touch the ground.
Ladybug, ladybug, tie your shoe.
Ladybug, ladybug, land on blue.

Connie R. Ion

I'm a Little Ladybug

Sung to: "I'm a Little Teapot"

I'm a little ladybug on the go
Landing on an arm, now an elbow.
See me fly around and around your hand,
Now watch as on your thumb I land.

I'm a little ladybug searching for some toes,
But watch me quickly land on your nose.
Now I look around and head for your hair,
I muss it up a bit, then pat it down with care.

I'm a little ladybug looking for a knee,
I'm just so happy you're not bugged by me.
Now you see me heading for your chest,
This little ladybug needs some rest.

Have your children use their fingers as "ladybugs" to act out the movements described in the song.

Susan M. Paprocki

My Ladybug

Sung to: "Twinkle, Twinkle, Little Star"

My ladybug, how I love you.
You're round and red and tiny, too.
Little black spots all over your shell,
You crawl and fly so very well.
Oh, oh, oh, look at you go!
Flying high and crawling low.

Margo S. Hunter

Worm Garden

They're wiggly and slimy, but worms are a vital part of a healthy garden. The work of millions of worms keep garden soil in good condition. Encourage your children to learn about the value of worms by observing them at work.

You Will Need

SUPPLIES

a large, clear-plastic or glass container (a 1-gallon jar works well)

a jar cover prepared with air holes

clump-free soil

lettuce leaves and apple peels

dark-colored fabric (or you can use a sheet, towel, or pillowcase)

about ten earthworms

water

worm food (explained on page 35)

Worms are good for gardens. Because they leave tiny burrows wherever they go, they help to increase the amount of air and water that gets into the soil. Worms also break down organic matter like leaves and grass into things that plants can use. And after worms eat, they leave behind "castings," a very valuable type of fertilizer. With all their eating and crawling, worms are the best at turning the soil, or bringing organic matter down from the top and mixing it with the soil below. There are many different types of worms. The most common is the pale red garden earthworm.

What to Do Fill your clear-plastic or glass gallon container about one-third full with lump-free dirt. Scatter a torn lettuce leaf and a few apple peelings on top, then cover with a little more dirt. Add more torn-up lettuce and apple peelings and another scoop of dirt. Add about 1 cup of water. Wait for the water to soak in. You want your new worm home to be damp but not wet.

Gently add about ten earthworms. Put on a tight-fitting cover so the worms cannot escape, but be sure to poke air holes so the worms can breathe. Cover the container with the dark-colored fabric so the top of the container (where the air holes are) remains open. Put your worm home in a shady, cool place.

When you want to view your worms at work, remove the fabric covering and watch. When you add food, be sure to poke it into the earth near the side of the container so you can watch it disappear. Make sure the newly added food is covered with dirt.

Troubleshooting If your worms start to die, your worm home could be too wet, too dry, or too hot. Feel the contents and see. Try changing the location of the worm container. If your worm home smells rotten, chances are the contents are too wet or some unsuitable food was added.

About Worm Food

Worms love potato peelings, carrots, lettuce, cabbage, celery, banana peels, orange rinds, grapefruit and other fruit peelings, cornmeal, oatmeal, crushed eggshells, used coffee grinds (and the filter), and used tea bags. Chopping the foods makes it easier for worms to eat. Whenever the soil in your worm home starts to feel dry, add a little water. Earthworms can drown in too much water, so just add a little. Worms do not like meat, fish, oily food, or dairy products such as butter and cheese. In fact, these foods will make your worm home smelly.

Worm Bin

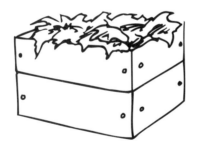

Did you know that one thousand worms—that's about one pound—will eat one-half to one pound of food scraps each day? You can make a worm bin in which worms will multiply rapidly while eating your organic food waste and turning it into healthy soil. Plastic, commercially-made worm bins are available, or you can make your own from wood. For complete instructions, ask your local cooperative extension office, solid waste company, or visit your library. Basically, a bedding of newspaper, water, soil, and worm food will get you started. Red worms are best for this type of project.

What Kids Can Do
Your children can help with many parts of the worm home! Feeding the worms could become part of the monthly chore chart.

The Dirt on Gardening

WORM FACTS

- An earthworm is usually about 4 inches long. The largest earthworm ever found was in South Africa. It measured 22 feet from its nose to the tip of its tail!

- Worms really don't have noses, legs, arms, or eyes. They do have a front end with a fleshy band around it, called an anterior, and a back end, called a posterior.

- Although worms don't have eyes, they are sensitive to light. If exposed to light too long (about one hour), worms can become paralyzed.

- Worms can grow a new tail if it is cut off, but not a new head.

- If a worm's skin dries out, it will die.

- Worms are cold-blooded animals.

- Baby worms hatch from eggs. Egg capsules begin growing under the fleshy band near an earthworm's head. The capsule slips out from the band, moves along the worm's body to the front of its head where the eggs drop off. Baby worms are white and threadlike.

- Baby earthworms become adults in three months. They can live up to four years.

Worms

Observing Worms

Set an earthworm on top of some soil and let your children observe it. How does the earthworm move? What color is it? What does its skin feel like? What does the worm do? Explain that earthworms hatch from eggs that are inside a cocoon in the soil. Many tiny worms hatch from a single cocoon. An earthworm's face has just one feature: a mouth, with which it eats soil and decaying plants. Near the opening of the worm's tunnel, little piles of digested food, called castings, can be seen.

Worm Tracks

Let your children dip 6-inch pieces of string into brown tempera paint and then pull the strings across pieces of white paper to make "worm" tracks. Encourage them to make their strings crawl and wiggle like real worms.

Earthworm Movement

Help your children notice how worms move. They scrunch their muscles up and then stretch them out. Let your children practice moving like worms. Since worms sleep during the day and come out at night, turn out the lights and ask your "worms" to move all around. When you turn on the lights, have the "worms" pretend to sleep. Turn out the lights again so your "worms" can do their important work.

Extension: Explain to your children that earthworms cannot see, hear, or smell, but they can feel vibrations. To demonstrate, have the children lie down quietly on the floor. Stomp your feet on the floor as hard as you can. Did they feel the floor move? Those little vibrations are the same vibrations a worm feels when it is underground.

Worm Finger Puppet

Set out small paper cups and sheets of brown tissue paper or construction paper. Help each child make a finger-sized hole in the bottom of his or her cup. Let them tear the brown paper into tiny pieces and fill their cups half full. To work the puppet, have your children hold their cup in one hand while they stick the index finger of the other hand up through the hole in the bottom of the cup. Have children use their worm puppets to surprise their friends and family as they recite the rhyme below.

Willie the Worm

I have a pet named Willy,
Who lives at home with me.
I keep him in this special cup
So all my friends can see.

Where, oh, where is Willy?
Oh, where can Willy be?
Come out now, little Willy,
So all my friends can see.

He is a little shy.
I must be very firm.
Come out now, little Willy!
Come out, my Willy Worm!

Have children keep their index fingers hidden under the torn paper "dirt" while they recite the rhyme. At the end of the rhyme, have them push their fingers up out of the paper to show their little wiggly worm.

Jean Warren

Did You Ever See an Earthworm?

Sung to: "Did You Ever See a Lassie?"

Did you ever see an earthworm,
An earthworm, an earthworm?
Did you ever see an earthworm
Move this way and that?
Move this way and that way,
Move this way and that way.
Did you ever see an earthworm
Move this way and that?

Have your children move their fingers, arms, or bodies like earthworms as they sing the song.

Betty Silkunas

Hummingbird Garden

The small, quick-flying hummingbird captivates the attention of all ages. If you and your children provide the right environment with lots of sweet nectar, hummingbirds will linger for you to enjoy and study.

You Will Need

STARTS
any number of the following:

- scarlet sage (salvia)
- petunia (a red variety like comanche would be best)
- bee balm
- hollyhocks

for the hanging planter, any number of the following:

- patience plant (red or pink impatiens)
- lady's eardrops (fuchsias)

SUPPLIES
basic gardening tools

Soil and Location Fertile, well-drained soil in full sun for the garden. Shade or partial shade for the hanging planter.

Space Try to plant the garden near a place in partial shade where a planter and hummingbird feeder can hang.

Time Required Depending on the maturity of your starts, allow two to five weeks to begin attracting hummingbirds.

Planting the Garden Depending on the selected location, arrange the garden with the tallest plants in the back and the shortest plants in the front. Hollyhocks can grow to 6 feet, so plant them in the background first. Follow with bee balm, salvia, and then petunias. Bee balm can spread if allowed to remain in the ground over winter. Unlike many evasive plants, bee balm is easily removed if you no longer want it in the same location, or it can be readily transplanted to a new location.

Planting the Hanging Planter You can plant both impatiens and fuchsias together, or put all impatiens in one basket and fuchsias in another.

Care Hanging planters need regular watering to prevent them from drying out. Pluck old blossoms off fuchsias and petunias to ensure longer blooming time.

What Kids Can Do
Your children can help plant the starts, water, and weed. They will enjoy mixing nectar (see recipe on page 40) and filling a hummingbird feeder. Let them help you look up the kinds of hummingbirds they can expect to see in their garden.

More Ideas Hummingbirds like tubular flowers that are orange, red, and pink. The ideal Hummingbird Garden will have a variety of flowers, plants, shrubs, and trees, blooming from mid- to late-April through the summer season. Some additional plants you might include are these: vines—honeysuckle, morning glory, and trumpet creeper; shrubs—rhododendrons, butterfly bushes, and flowering quince; flowers—montbretia *(Crocosmia),* cardinal flower, columbine, coralbells, geranium, and begonia.

Hummingbird Facts

- The world has about 340 species of hummingbirds.

- At 2¼ inches long, the Cuban bee hummingbird is the world's smallest bird—about the size of a bumblebee!

> **Tip**
> Apply petroleum jelly around the feeder openings to discourage flies, bees, and wasps from being attracted to the nectar.

- The hummingbird is the only bird that can fly backward. They also can hover like helicopters and move forward and sideways.

- A hummingbird's fast-beating wings actually hum and can beat from 20 to 200 times per second.

- These small birds can travel great distances. For example, the ruby-throated hummingbird, which weighs about one tenth of an ounce, travels 600 miles in migration.

- A hummingbird drinks nectar by placing its open bill into a flower and licking up the nectar. The bird's tongue, which actually divides into two lobes at its end, extends beyond the tip of its long bill and can reach deep into a flower to drink nectar at a rate of about 13 licks per second.

- Hummingbirds also eat tiny insects and spiders.

- Ounce for ounce, hummingbirds use more calories than almost any other warm-blooded animal. They may drink up to eight times their body weight daily.

- Hummingbirds usually build cup-shaped nests from moss, seed down, and spider webs. Each female lays about two tiny eggs.

The Dirt on Gardening

ABOUT HUMMINGBIRD FEEDERS

- For success in attracting hummingbirds, hang feeders among flowers hummingbirds naturally like, well out of the reach of potentially dangerous cats. If you doubt that there is enough red about, tie a red ribbon on the feeder.

- Because hummingbirds can be territorial and defend flowers and feeders within their favorite roosting spot, put two or more feeders out of sight of one another.

- Each year, feeders should be put up in time for the arrival of hummingbirds in your area. This migration time varies depending on where you live. For information, consult your local Audubon Society.

- Change the nectar every three to four days and clean the feeders regularly with hot water, never harsh detergent. This should prevent mold, which will appear as black spots inside your feeder. If you do see mold, remove it immediately with a scrub brush or add some sand with the hot water, and shake the feeder until the mold is removed.

Hummingbirds

Making Nectar

Hummingbirds prefer the following nectar recipe over commercial instant mixes. For one or two minutes, boil one part granulated sugar with four parts water. Cool the mixture and store it in the refrigerator. Never use honey, artificial sweeteners, or red food coloring, as all of these can be harmful to hummingbirds. Add the nectar to a hummingbird feeder and hang it near a window. Your children will delight in watching the little birds enjoy their nectar.

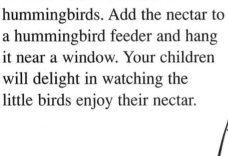

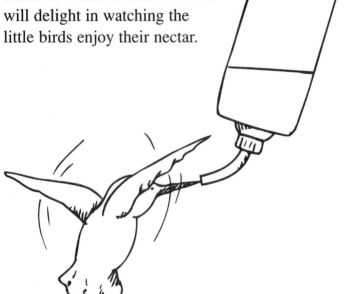

Big or Little

On a flannelboard, place felt cutouts of four or five different sizes of birds. Ask your children to line the birds up according to their size, from the smallest to the largest. Set your flannelboard out so that your children can play with the bird cutouts on their own.

Dance of the Hummingbirds

Discuss hummingbirds with your group. Show them pictures of hummingbirds from bird books or magazines. Ask if anyone has ever seen a hummingbird. What did it look like? How big was it? Talk about how hummingbirds stick their long beaks into flowers to gather a sweet liquid called nectar.

Show your children how to hold their arms up and flap their hands rapidly to imitate a hummingbird. Set out chairs to represent flowers and let your children pretend to be hummingbirds stealing the nectar from the flowers.

Busy Little Hummingbird
Sung to: "Mary Had a Little Lamb"

Busy little hummingbird,
Hummingbird, hummingbird.
Busy little hummingbird
Flying all around.

Sipping nectar everywhere,
Everywhere, everywhere.
Sipping nectar everywhere
With a humming sound.

Mmm, mmm . . . etc.

Continue humming another verse of the song.

Jean Warren

Nine Little Hummingbirds
Sung to: "Ten Little Indians"

One little, two little, three little hummingbirds,
Four little, five little, six little hummingbirds,
Seven little, eight little, nine little hummingbirds,
Flying all around.

Nine little, eight little, seven little hummingbirds,
Six little, five little, four little hummingbirds,
Three little, two little, one little hummingbird,
Making humming sounds.

Jean Warren

See the Little Hummingbirds
Sung to: "Someone's in the Kitchen With Dinah"

See the little hummingbird hover,
See the little hummingbird dip, dip, dip, dip,
See the little hummingbird hover,
Yummy nectar, sip, sip, sip!

Jean Warren

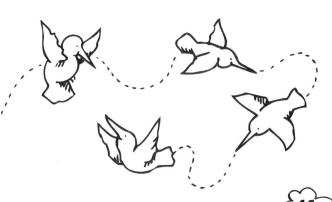

Bird Sanctuary

Check with your local Fish and Wildlife Department for specific information about your native wildlife. It should be able to provide you with information on what kind of birds you will attract, and what native plants you should use.

You Will Need

PLANTS

trees: vine maple *(Acer circinatum)*, huckleberry *(Vaccinium ovatum)*, red-twig dogwood *(Cornus sericea)*

shrubs: apple serviceberry *(Amelanchier x grandiflora)*, mock orange *(Philadelphus lewisii)*, blueberry elder *(Sambucus caerulea)*, Oregon grape *(Mahonia aquifolium)*, California wax myrtle *(Myrica californica)*, red flowering current *(Ribes sanguineum)*

ground covers: sword fern *(Polystichum munitum)*, kinnikinnick *(Arctostaphylos uva-ursi)*

SUPPLIES

basic gardening tools

birdhouse

birdbath

Soil and Location Your Bird Sanctuary will need average to well-drained soil and a sunny area with some shade available. Planting the garden in an area with existing trees will bring shade, or include some small trees when planning your Bird Sanctuary.

Space You can use your whole outdoor area to attract birds, or arrange groupings of plants near windows so you and your children can enjoy the birds while indoors.

Time Required You will most likely start to attract birds as soon as you provide them with the four basic elements of habitat, food, water, and shelter.

Habitat The most inviting habitat for birds is one with trees, shrubs, and ground covers—plants at every level. This provides a safe environment for the birds. Select a few plants in each category from the plant list provided. If you already have downed logs in your outdoor area, be sure to keep them as they provide great shelter for cavity nesters. If you do not have a log, consider adding one to the landscape!

Bird Feeders Having one or two bird feeders in your habitat is crucial. You can use tube, platform, or suet block feeders. (Because suet melts in warm weather, use suet feeders only in the cooler months of the year.) Make sure you place the feeders where they are safe from cats and squirrels, but also in an area where you can enjoy watching the wildlife. Check your library for the kinds of foods appropriate for the species of birds in your area.

Birdbaths and Other Water Features Your water source can be something as simple as a rock with an indentation in it, or it can be a traditional, store-bought birdbath. The safest kind of birdbath has a pedestal base, which cats and squirrels cannot climb. If you are more ambitious, there are kits available to create a pond. No matter which option you choose, the birds will love to splash around in the water.

Make sure the water source is near a perch and in an open area so that the birds can dry themselves while still safe from predators. The water in your water source should be no more than 3 inches deep—birds can drown in deeper water. To give the birds a spot in which to lounge, place a rock that points out above the water in the bath. To keep the water warm during the winter months, use a heating element (found at pet supply stores).

What Kids Can Do
Your children can help plant the garden, fill birdbaths and feeders, and observe the birds.

Moving water is more attractive to wildlife than still water. Add a dripper to your birdbath, or place a mister in a tree (hummingbirds especially like to fly through the mist).

Birdhouses Birds like weathered, unpainted wood that reminds them of natural nesting sites—the thicker the wood, the better the insulation. Make sure there is ventilation at the top and bottom of the house. The size of the opening determines what kind of bird you will attract. A 1 ¼- to 1 ½-inch hole is small enough to keep out starlings, yet large enough to be used by other desirable birds like swallows, wrens, chickadees, finches, and nuthatches. You should be able to get inside the house to clean it once a year, preferably in early spring.

Care Birds do not require a perfectly groomed yard. However, birdbaths and feeders will need to be refilled and cleaned. Clean and disinfect your birdbaths during the hot summer months, especially. It is a good idea to do this at least weekly, if possible, to remove the slime that breeds bacteria and viruses. A good birdbath and feeder disinfectant is a mixture of one part bleach to seven parts water. Pour the solution into your empty birdbath, and let it stand for a few minutes. Wash the birdbath thoroughly using a stiff brush to scrub the scum from all surfaces. Rinse the birdbath well and refill with clean water.

The Dirt on Gardening

Providing water is essential in a Bird Sanctuary. A simple water source can be made by placing a clean garbage can lid on top of two bricks. Fill the lid with no more than three inches of water. If the surface is slippery, add a small flat rock or piece of flagstone to the container. To help birds find your water source, try hanging a hose overhead and letting water drip into the container. Birds are very attuned to the sound of falling water.

Variations: Place a clean 20-inch plant saucer (available at garden stores) on top of a plastic milk crate. You can even use a clean baking pan (minimum 9-by-13-inches) on a flat railing. Secure the baking pan with bungee cords so it will not fall off. It is also possible to use a clean kitty litter box set atop a bucket (put a rock in the bucket for stability).

Birds

Bird Nests

Give your children brown paper lunch sacks. Then take them on a walk and let them collect items that a bird might use to make a nest, such as twigs, leaves, pieces of string, etc. After the walk, have the children fold down the sides of their bags to form "nests." Have them set their bags outside so that the birds can use the contents for nest building.

Baby Birds

Sit in a circle with your children. Have them pretend that they are baby birds. Encourage them to chirp. Pretend to bring them all juicy worms. Next, show them how to flap their wings and fly out of the nest. Explain what a brave feat this must be when a baby bird flies for the first time. Continue until everyone has had a turn.

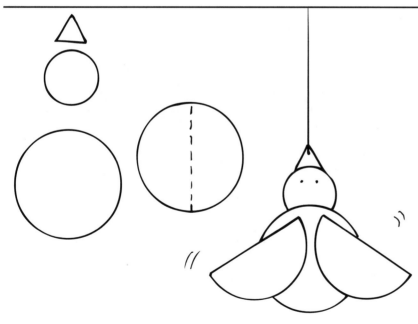

Bird Mobile

For each child, cut two large circles and one small circle out of construction paper. Have the children glue or tape the small circle to the large circle as shown in the illustration. Next, have them cut the remaining circle in half and glue it to the middle of the large circle, as shown, to make wings. Next, have your children glue on small triangles for beaks. Make a hole at the top of each bird, and hang the birds from the ceiling with string.

Song of the Birds
Sung to: "Up on the Housetop"

Out in the yard, I hear their song,
Chirping happily all day long.
Building their nests with grass and twigs,
Hunting for worms and tasty seeds.

Cheep, cheep, cheep,
Hear their song.
Cheep, cheep, cheep,
All day long.

Out in the yard, all day long,
Working hard, while singing their song.

Jean Warren

Five Little Birds
Cut five bird shapes out of felt. Place one bird at a time on a flannelboard as you read the counting rhyme below.

One little bird flying in the blue,
Along comes another, now there are two.

Two little birds perched up in a tree,
Along comes another, now there are three.

Three little birds, see them swoop and soar,
Along comes another, now there are four.

Four little birds, through the skies they dive,
Along comes another, now there are five.

Diane Thom

Little Bluebird
Sung to: "Twinkle, Twinkle, Little Star"

Little bluebird, flying around,
Up to the sky, then down to the ground.
Little bluebird, flapping your wings,
Little bluebird, gently sing.
Little bluebird, fly to your nest,
Now it is time to take a rest.

Have your children pretend to be bluebirds and act out the motions described in the song.

Susan M. Paprocki

Short and Tall Garden

Plant this garden to help reinforce the concepts of short and tall.

You Will Need

STARTS

short plants: ageratum *(Ageratum houstonianum)*, lamb's-ear *(Stachys byzantina)*, sweet alyssum *(Lobularia maritima)*, carpet bugle *(Ajuga reptans)*, wax begonia *(Begonia semperflorens)*, impatiens *(Impatiens wallerana)*

tall plants: astilbe *(Astilbe arendsii)*, larkspur *(Consolida ambigua)*, mixed snapdragons *(Antirrhinum majus)*, sunflower *(Helianthus)*, black-eyed Susan *(Rudbeckia hirta)*

SUPPLIES

basic gardening tools

compost and other organic matter

Soil and Location You can plant your Short and Tall Garden anywhere you please, as long as you choose an area with average, well-drained soil.

Space You will need a 5-foot-by-5-foot plot of soil.

Time Required This garden will take just the time it takes to prepare the area and plant the starts. Your children should be able to see the height differences almost right away.

Planting the Garden Prepare the soil with compost and other organic matter, then lay out the starts. Arrange the tall plants in the back section of your garden, and place the short plants in front.

Care You will need to water, feed, and weed your Short and Tall Garden. In addition, you will need to deadhead the ageratum, larkspur, snapdragon, and sweet alyssum flowers to promote more flower production.

What Kids Can Do

Take your children and a list of the plants you have selected from the list on page 46 to your local nursery. Your children will get to see many other tall and short plants. They can also help plant, weed, and deadhead flowers.

Did You Know?

You can use grass clippings to mulch between garden rows, or on any plant, to help retain moisture and cut down on weeds.

Tips

Lamb's-ear starts out as a short plant, then it sends out tall spikes with small lavender-colored flowers.

The Dirt on Gardening

PRE-GERMINATING SEEDS

Pre-germinated seeds are seeds that are sprouted before you sow them. Some seeds germinate easier if soaked in water for 12 hours before being planted outdoors. Seeds that do well when pre-germinated include

beans, beets, corn, morning glory, peas (edible and sweet), Swiss chard, and spinach. You can pre-germinate seeds for planting or just for observation. Once the seeds have germinated, show your children the shoot growing up one side of the seed. The shoot will become the stem of the plant.

To pre-germinate seeds, soak them for 12 hours in room-temperature water. Spread two layers of dampened paper towels on a flat surface. Place your seeds about 1 inch apart, and carefully roll up the paper towels. Use a rubber band to keep each towel in the shape of a tube, and label it with the name of the seeds inside. Place the rolls in a plastic bag, and label it as well. Loosely close the bag—the seeds need air to germinate. Most seed packets will list how long germination takes, but you and your children can sneak a peek at them each day. Some seeds can take up to a week to germinate, so be patient. Check to see if the rolls are drying out, and dampen them if they need it. When little roots start to show, your sprouts are ready for planting in rows using the Seed Goop Method (see page 27).

Short and Tall

Only One Me

Sometimes I'm short.
Sometimes I'm tall.
Sometimes I'm big.
Sometimes I'm small.

Something is wrong.
There's only one me—
So do I stretch?
How can this be?

It really is simple.
I stay the same.
It depends who I'm next to—
I don't really change.

I'm big and tall
Standing next to my brother.
But I'm short and small
When I'm next to my mother.

So when someone asks
Are you short or tall?
I just say "yes!"
Then nothing at all.

Jean Warren

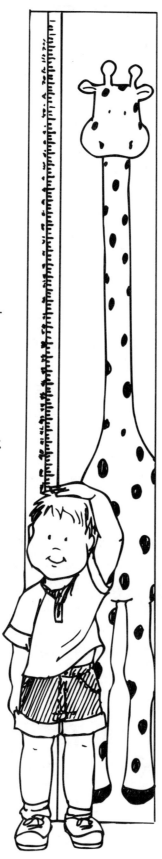

Who's Tall?

Demonstrate to your children the difference between tall and short. Pick two children and have them stand side by side. Who is the tallest? Who is the shortest? To show that size is relative, be sure to pick the tallest child and compare him or her to yourself.

Extension: Try to lead your children into a discussion about the advantages of being very short or very tall. What would they do? What would they see?

Counting Fun

Take your children out to your Short and Tall Garden, and have them help you count each tall flower and each short flower. Which group has the most flowers?

Short-Tall Dramatics

Have your children pretend they are all very short. Ask them to help you make up an adventure such as "Out in the Garden" or "On the Playground." What would your children see and do in the garden or playground? Another time, have your children pretend they are all very tall. What adventures could they have? Where would they go? What would they see? How could they help others?

Flower Patterning

Outdoors or in a planter box, place four to six plastic or silk flowers in a pattern, such as tall-short-short-tall-short-short. Have your children use additional flowers to continue the pattern. Be sure that you have equal numbers of short- and long-stemmed flowers.

Up and Down Garden

Some plants naturally grow by trailing down or crawling up. Planting and tending to this garden will help you reinforce the concept of up and down.

You Will Need

SEEDS OR STARTS

plants that grow up: cardinal climber *(Ipomoea x multifida)*, morning glory *(Ipomoea)*, runner bean *(Phaseolus coccineus)*, sweet pea *(Lathyrus odoratus)*

plants that grow down: licorice plant *(Helichrysum petiolare)*, trailing lobelia *(Lobelia erinus)*, nasturtium *(Tropaeolum majus)*, verbena *(Verbena x hybrida)*

SUPPLIES

long wooden, plastic, or bamboo poles (or a small trellis)

time-release fertilizer

plant ties (see "Did You Know?" on page 51)

Soil and Location Your Up and Down Garden will need at least six hours of sun and well-drained soil. You can start in the springtime, a few weeks after all danger of frost is past.

Space This garden can be grown in a raised bed or in containers.

Time Required Buy starts to begin enjoying this garden right away. If you use seeds, it will take four to eight weeks to see the plants crawl up the trellis or spill out of the bed or container.

Planting the Garden If you are using a container, follow the directions for the Container Garden on pages 70 and 71. Add the "up" plants to the middle of the bed or container along with a pole or a small trellis. Morning glory, sweet pea, runner bean, and cardinal creeper have tendrils that will wind themselves around the pole or trellis—you and your children just need to guide them along. Your stakes or trellis should be about a third longer than the mature plant is expected to be. The extra third is the portion that goes into the soil, close to the stem of your plant. Staking a plant while it is growing is easier because the branches are a little more flexible and less likely to break than they are when fully grown. For a natural pole for your plants to climb up, you can use sunflowers. The stems are quite sturdy and "hairy," which will make it easy for the plants to climb up. Add your "down" plants all around the sunflowers, making sure that they are close enough to the rim of the bed or container to grow down over the edge.

Care Your Up and Down Garden will need to be watered and deadheaded on a regular basis, and the "up" plants will need to be tied up as they continue to grow.

Did You Know?

Plants that can be easily blown over by the wind or that get top-heavy with blossoms or fruit need to be supported on stakes with plant ties. To gently train your plants up a stake, you can make plant ties out of anything soft and pliable. Some examples are garden twine, string, narrow strips of cloth, used pantyhose, or twist ties. The ties need to be long enough to wrap around the plant stem and tie into a knot behind the stake. To support the weight of the maturing plant, use plant ties every 10 to 12 inches along the stem.

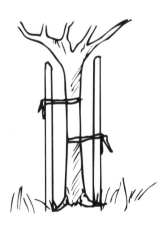

What Kids Can Do

Your children can help plant nasturtium seeds (they are large and can be easily poked into the soil), water the garden, and deadhead the wilted flowers.

The Dirt on Gardening

FERTILIZERS

Always check the ingredients listed on the container of the fertilizer you buy. It will have three numbers printed on the bag, which represent the ratio of nitrogen, phosphorus, and potassium in the fertilizer. They are often referred to as "NPK." Read the instruction label carefully. It will tell you when and how much to use.

Nitrogen: Nitrogen speeds growth, but too much will burn roots and prevent flowering. Too little nitrogen will make green leaves turn a lighter shade and cause older leaves to turn yellow. The best type of nitrogen-rich fertilizer should have the words "slow-release" printed on the label. It dissolves slowly so the plants do not get too much nitrogen at once. If you prefer a chemical-free fertilizer, organic compost will provide your plants with all the nitrogen they need.

Phosphorus: Phosphorus helps plants form new roots and develop seeds, fruits, and flowers. Plants that are not getting enough phosphorus will have darker old leaves or develop a reddish color. When they need phosphorus, plants will start to produce smaller, less healthy flowers and fruit. Because it tends to stay in one spot, phosphorous should be added to the soil when you are tilling.

Potassium: Potassium increases a plant's disease resistance, makes the stems strong, and keeps it growing vigorously. Plants with too little potassium will have a general slowing of growth and leaves that are smaller than usual.

FERTILIZING SEEDLINGS

The time to fertilize seedlings is when you notice that the second set of leaves have unfurled. Purchase concentrated, water-soluble fertilizer specially made for seedlings. The fertilizer should have the numbers 10-52-10 or 10-30-10 on the label. The directions usually require ½ teaspoon of fertilizer to 4 cups of water. However, this mixture is too strong for seedlings and will burn them. Instead, mix just ¼ teaspoon of fertilizer in 8 cups of water. To store the fertilizer, mix it in a clean, 2-liter soda bottle that has a lid. After using the fertilizer, label it with a permanent marker, and keep it tightly capped. Keep all fertilizers and any other gardening chemicals out of the reach of children.

Up and Down

Hands Up High
Sung to: "The Farmer in the Dell"

We raise our hands up high.
We raise our hands up high.
We give our hands a clap, clap, clap.
They almost reach the sky.

We move our hands down low.
We move our hands down low.
We give our hands a clap, clap, clap.
And then back up they go.

Jean Warren

Stair Steps
One of the best ways to help children understand the concept of up and down is to catch them as they are going up or down stairs and verbalize their actions: "Johann's going up." "Look, Chloe is coming down." Teach your children the song to the right to sing as they go up or down stairs.

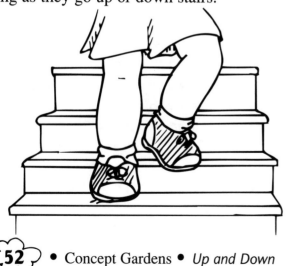

Roll the Dice
If you happen to have stairs available at your school, a fun game to play is called "Roll the Dice." Have each child roll a die and go up the number of stairs indicated on the die. To win, a child must roll enough "numbers" to go all the way up the stairs and all the way down. This game works best with small groups of children.

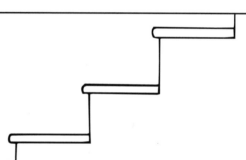

I Am Climbing
Sung to: "Frère Jacques"

I am climbing, I am climbing,
Up, up, up; up, up, up.
I will come to a stop, I will come to a stop,
At the top, at the top.

I am climbing, I am climbing,
Down, down, down; down, down, down.
I keep right on going, I keep right on going,
To the ground, to the ground.

Jean Warren

Observation Walk

Take your children outside for an up-down walk. First, have them look up and call out all the things they see that are up above their heads. Next, have them look down and name what they see by their feet.

A Ride in the Sky

Place small airplanes outside or in the block area. Encourage your children to take the planes for "rides" up in the "sky." Catch the children in action and have them tell you what is happening, such as, "The plane is flying up in the sky," or "Now the plane is coming down to land."

Upside-Down Cake

For snacktime, bring in a pineapple upside-down cake that is still in the pan. Explain to your children that the fruit was baked on the bottom of the cake, but it is supposed to be on top when the cake comes out of the pan. Ask your children if they can figure out how to make things right. Hopefully, someone will say, "Turn the cake upside down." If none of the children suggest that option, suggest it yourself. Let your children watch you flip the cake over onto a plate so that what is supposed to be up is up and what is supposed to be down is down.

Here We Go

During circle time, have your children pretend to be airplanes flying up and down. Sing the song below together.

Sung to: "Frère Jacques"

Here we go, here we go,
Way up high, way up high.
We are little airplanes.
We are little airplanes,
In the sky, in the sky.

Here we go, here we go,
Zoom down low, zoom down low.
We are little airplanes.
We are little airplanes.
Watch us go, watch us go.

Jean Warren

Sensory Garden

What better way to get kids interested in nature than to have a garden full of plants that have interesting textures and smells?

You Will Need

STARTS

"smelly" plants: Daphne (*Cneorum*), heliotrope (*Heliotropium arborescens*), many species of lavender (*Lavandula*), stock (*Matthiola*), sweet pea (*Lathyrus odoratus*), thyme (*Thymus x citriodorus*), peppermint or rose scented geraniums (*Pelargonium tomentosum or graveolens*), sweet basil (*Ocimum basilicum*)

"feely" plants: artichoke (plant at least two), sea holly (*Eryngium amethystinum*), lamb's-ear (*Stachys byzantina*), Heliotrope (*Heliotropium arborescens*), snow-in-summer (*Cerastium tomentosum*)

SUPPLIES

basic gardening tools

stakes and plant ties for sweet peas (see page 51 for details)

Soil and Location You will need an area that receives at least six hours of sunlight and has good drainage. You can start planting most plants soon after the last frost. Wait until later to plant basil, which needs night temperatures in or above the 50s.

Space To get a good representation of sensory plants, you will need at least a 5-foot-by-5-foot plot. If you're short on space, many of the plants can be grown in containers surrounding your Sensory Garden.

Time Required Since you will be using plant starts, you should be able to enjoy the textures and aromas right away.

Planting the Garden After deciding where to plant your Sensory Garden, prepare the soil as you would for any other garden. Then choose a few of you and your children's favorite plants from each list. Arrange the plants according to height, with taller ones toward the back and shorter ones in front. Mix textures and colors throughout the garden. Make sure you allow enough space for each plant to grow. Stock, sweet peas, and scented geraniums are all good candidates for growing in containers. You and your children can enjoy feeling and smelling the plants as they grow in the garden, or you can cut some flowers to make a fragrant bouquet to enjoy indoors.

Care Your Sensory Garden will need to be watered and the faded flowers deadheaded. Harvest one artichoke while the bud is tight and plump. Leave the other artichoke on the stem, and it will produce a spectacular thistlelike, purple-blue flower.

The Dirt on Gardening

ANNUAL OR PERENNIAL?

Annuals complete their life cycles in one year. They germinate, grow, flower, produce seed, and then die. Usually they are from warm or tropical areas and cannot survive the winter in colder climates. Annuals can bloom for months.

Perennials are non-woody plants that live for more than two years. Although many perennials are from the evergreen family, some are considered "herbaceous," which means they will die back to the ground during the winter months, but come back the next season. Perennials usually bloom for two to four weeks.

For More Fun

Many of the plants listed on page 54 have colorful flowers to look at, and you can taste the artichokes and thyme. To complete the other five senses, add fountain grass *(Pennisetum alopecuroides)* to your garden. Let your children listen for the grass rustling in the breeze.

What Kids Can Do

If you are ordering plants from a catalog, your children can look at the pictures and pick plants they like from the list. Or, you can take them to a nursery where they can feel and smell the plants for themselves and then decide which ones they like. Your children can also help tend the garden by watering, weeding, and deadheading.

Smelling and Feeling

Smelling Socks

Collect several clean socks and an assortment of fragrant items. You might choose such items as cedar blocks, potpourri, scented votive candles, and cotton balls scented with a flavoring extract. Place an item in the toe of each sock. Knot the tops of the socks to seal the items inside. Let your children take turns smelling the socks. Which scents can they recognize? Which scents do they like best?

Texture Detectives

At circle time, play a texture game. Ask two or three children to go out of the circle and search for something soft. Discuss the objects brought back to the circle. Why are they soft? Continue by asking other children to find objects that are rough, smooth, hard, etc.

The Nose Knows

Challenge your children with a matching game. Collect several small plastic margarine tubs. Poke holes in the lids. Place a different-smelling item in each container. Peanut butter, lemon sections, cinnamon, and diced onions are just a few possibilities. Next, cut from magazines or draw pictures of each item. Place each of the pictures on a separate index card and cover with clear self-stick paper for durability. Mix up the containers and the pictures. Let your children take turns matching the container with the correct picture. Remember to clean out the containers at the end of each day.

The Smelling Song

Sung to: "It's Raining, It's Pouring"

I'm smelling, I'm smelling,
My nose is busy smelling.
This is the song I like to sing,
When I smell most anything!

Kathy McCullough

Sweet-Smelling Art

For a special sensory experience, add a few drops of peppermint, lemon, or vanilla extract to your children's next batch of modeling dough. Or, have your children draw pictures with scented markers. Encourage them to exchange pictures and compare scents.

"Feelie" Bag

Find four to six different textures of fabric, such as silk, flannel, corduroy, wool, and denim. Cut out two 6-by-6-inch squares of each fabric. Place the squares in a bag. Let your children take turns reaching into the bag and pulling out a square. After feeling the square and describing how it feels, have the child reach in again and try to find the matching square.

Texture Snacks

Whenever you have snacks, take the time to point out the texture and the smell of each food. Some examples include smooth, cold, sweet yogurt; hard, crunchy carrots; slippery, mushy peas; and bumpy, salty popcorn.

Rainbow Garden

Flowering plants bloom in a palette of colors. With so many different kinds to choose from, your children can grow a rainbow and learn about colors, too!

You Will Need

SEEDS OR STARTS
any number of the following for each color:

red: red sage (*Salvia splendens*) or red zinnia (*Zinnia elegans*)

orange: orange zinnia (*Zinnia elegans*) or California poppy (*Eschscholzia californica*)

yellow: yellow marigold (*Tagestes erecta*) or yellow calendula (*Calendula officinalis*)

green: bells-of-Ireland (*Moluccella laevis*), quaking grass, or any green herb of your choice

blue: blue bachelor's button (*Centaurea cyanus*) or larkspur (*Delphinium consolida*)

purple: purple petunias (*Petunia x hybrida*) or violas (*Viola x wittrockiana*)

SUPPLIES
basic gardening tools

Soil and Location Fertile, well-drained soil in full sun.

Space Allow enough room between rows so weeding can be easily done. If you want to make a rainbow without space between the colors, plant all six rows as tightly together as possible so weeding and care can be done from each side.

Time Required For direct seeding, anticipate approximately 70 to 100 days. With starts, allow approximately 30 to 60 days. The suggested plants are all annuals and should bloom at the same time. If you vary from the recommended list, check the maturation dates.

Planting the Garden Plant your garden so the rainbow colors are in order: red, orange, yellow, green, blue, and purple. Follow the directions on seed packages for direct sowing, or carefully transplant starts in marked areas.

Many of the common flowers suggested come in a variety of colors or mixes. To make the Rainbow Garden successful, seeds and starts need to be one specific color. Of course, there are many variations of a color as well. Try to keep your red colors a true red instead of rose or maroon.

Care With seeds, thin according to package directions when the seedlings reach the recommended height. For both seeds and starts, weed, water, and deadhead as needed.

Harvesting This is a garden to enjoy outdoors. If your garden produces abundant blooms, take cuttings and bring your rainbow indoors.

Best for Young Hands

Your children can help with many parts of this garden! Have them help plant the seeds or starts, water, weed, and deadhead. Let them mark the rows with colored markers so they know what to expect (see "The Dirt on Gardening" section to the right.)

For More Fun

- Try planting your Rainbow Garden in curved rows that resemble a rainbow shape. Remember to plan for how the garden will be weeded and cared for.

- If you do not have enough space to plant a Rainbow Garden, plant the starts or seeds in containers and arrange them in rainbow color order.

- Just for fun, add a row or container of white and pink flowers. Good annuals to use include the shasta daisy or alyssum for white and cosmos, larkspur, or petunia for pink.

Tips

Terra cotta pots can easily be covered with tempera paint to make color-coded planters for a container Rainbow Garden. Have your children paint each of six terra cotta pots a different color of the rainbow. The children should paint each pot only on the outside and about two inches down on the inside.

The Dirt on Gardening

MARKERS

Garden markers show what is expected to grow in each row of a garden. Beginning gardeners will benefit from markers that picture what type of plant to look for when true leaves emerge and weeding needs to be done.

To make a simple marker, trim off any ragged edges from an empty seed packet. Cut a piece of clear self-stick paper twice as wide as the seed packet. Lay the packet facedown on one edge of the sticky side of the self-stick paper. Place a garden stake or craft stick on the back of the package so that 2 inches of the stick hangs below for placing into the ground. Fold the self-stick paper over the seed packet so that it covers the stake or stick and the rest of the packet.

For your Rainbow Garden, try making simple markers from strips of appropriately colored construction paper protected with self-stick paper.

Rainbows

Rainbow Colors

Cut a purple, a blue, a green, a yellow, an orange, and a red arc out of felt. Make each arc slightly larger than the one before it, so that the purple arc is the smallest, and the red arc is the largest. Then sing the song below and let the children create a rainbow by placing the appropriate colored arcs, one at a time, on a flannelboard.

Sung to: "Hush, Little Baby"

Rainbow purple, rainbow blue,
Rainbow green and yellow, too.
Rainbow orange, rainbow red,
Rainbow smiling overhead.

Come and count the colors with me.
How many colors can you see?
One, two, three, up to green,
Four, five, six colors can be seen.

Rainbow purple, rainbow blue,
Rainbow green and yellow, too.
Rainbow orange, rainbow red,
Rainbow smiling overhead.

Jean Warren

Color Celebration

Plan a color week. Each day, have your children come to school dressed in a different color. Plan scavenger hunts around your room searching for objects of a certain color. For snacktime, plan foods that are the color you are celebrating that day.

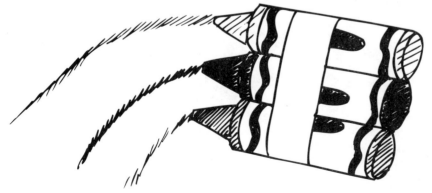

Color Arcs

Have each of your children choose three different-colored crayons. Help them tape the three crayons together in a line. Let your children use the taped crayons to draw colorful arcs on a piece of paper.

Here We Go
Sung to: "Here We Go Looby Loo"

Here we go looby loo,
Here we go looby light.
Here we go looby loo,
All on a Saturday night.

Children with blue shoes in,
Children with blue shoes out,
Children with blue shoes, shake, shake, shake,
And turn yourselves about.

Betty Silkunas

Invite your children to stand in a circle to sing this song. Continue with additional verses, each time naming a different shoe color, until all of the children have had an opportunity to stand in the center of the circle. You can also sing this song naming other items of clothing.

Rainbow Salad
Make a fruit salad that contains all the colors of the rainbow. Use strawberries, oranges, pineapple, green grapes, blueberries, and purple plums. Serve the salad with vanilla yogurt.

Colors That I Know
Sung to: "Twinkle, Twinkle, Little Star"

Yellow sunshine, soft green grass,
Orange pumpkin, small black bats.
Big blue sky, purple plums.
Red strawberries—yum, yum, yum!
Big brown tree trunks, bright white snow.
These are colors that I know.

Diane Thom

Bulb Garden

Add some color and fragrance to brighten the winter doldrums! Flowering bulbs make great gifts and decorations for the holidays!

You Will Need

If forcing bulbs in soil: tulip, daffodil, or crocus bulbs; potting soil; container (with drain hole in bottom)

If forcing bulbs in water: hyacinth bulbs; container that will hold just the base of the bulb in water

If forcing bulbs in pebbles: paperwhite bulbs; tall container; pebbles; garden stake; ribbon

SUPPLIES

basic gardening tools

There are three basic ways to force bulbs to grow indoors. The first is to trick bulbs into thinking it's time to bloom by refrigerating them for 8 to 12 weeks before planting them. (Hyacinth and paperwhites do not need the cooling process. Daffodils need 12 weeks of cooling, and tulips need 16 weeks.) The second is to simply place the bottom of a bulb in pebbles and add water. The third is to place a bulb in a container of pebbles.

Soil Method Crocus, daffodil, and tulip bulbs will bloom in any container from clay to china—just make sure the container has a drainage hole in the bottom. The size and number of bulbs you plant will determine the size of the container you need. You can place the bulbs as close as half an inch from the side of pot. Put a thin layer of pebbles on the bottom of the container, covering the drainage hole. Then fill the container half-full with a good potting soil. Place the bulbs in the container, pointed end up. Cover the bulbs with soil so that they just peak out the top. Water thoroughly. Label and date each container.

Store the bulbs in a dark area where the temperature is between 40 and 45 degrees Fahrenheit, such as a porch, garage, dry basement, or a spare refrigerator. You can use burlap or boxes to cover them if necessary. Keep the soil barely damp. When the bulbs send up shoots 2 to 3 inches high, move them to a sunny location to force them into bloom. For more fun, add grass seed a couple of weeks before tulips begin to bloom. This will add to the beauty and cover bare soil.

Water Method Hyacinths are the perfect bulbs for this method. They need to be placed in a container specially designed to hold just the bottom of a bulb in water, with room for the roots to grow. Or, you can use any container that is tapered at the top and will suspend the bulb in the water. Fill the glass so that the water just touches the bottom of the bulb. Replace the water when it becomes discolored, maintaining the same water level all the time. Place the container in a cool dark place until roots appear and the bulb produces a pointed growth on top. Then bring it into a well-lit area and watch it grow! It will take 6 to 8 weeks to bloom.

Pebble Method

Paperwhites can be grown in a container of pebbles and will bloom in just 4 to 6 weeks. You can store them in perforated bags in the refrigerator or in any cool, dark place until you are ready to plant them. If you want blooms at Christmas, start the

bulbs in mid-November. Fill a watertight container with a layer of pebbles. Set the bulbs on top and then fill in around with more pebbles so that the top of the bulb is still exposed. Add water until it reaches the base of the bulb. Place a stake near the bulb to support the flowers as they grow. Place the bulbs in a cool, dark area until you see roots growing in between the pebbles, usually after 2 to 3 weeks. Be sure to check the water occasionally and make sure the roots stay wet. When shoots start to emerge, bring the container into a cool location with bright, indirect exposure to sunlight for a week or so. Finally, move the bulbs into full sun. When the flowers get tall and floppy, tie them to the stake with some pretty ribbon.

What Kids Can Do

Your children can help fill the containers with soil, water, or pebbles; keep the bulbs watered; and observe the roots of the hyacinth bulbs as they grow in the water.

The Dirt on Gardening

WHAT IS THE DIFFERENCE BETWEEN BULBS AND SEEDS?

Seeds come in different sizes, shapes, and colors. Some can be eaten and some cannot. Some seeds germinate easily, while others need certain conditions to be met before they will germinate. Do you know that within every seed lives a tiny plant? You can hold in your hand 500 radishes, many thousands of petunias, or an entire meadow if you remember that each seed is a plant! Seeds can also travel. They cannot just get up and walk to a new location, but structures on the seed may allow it to move to a new location. Some of the moving forces might be wind, water, animals, and gravity.

A bulb is actually a package of immature leaves, stems, food, roots, and sometimes even flower buds. Onions, lilies, daffodils, and tulips are some of the plants grown from bulbs. If you cut a bulb in half, you can see the baby flower waiting to "hatch." Show your children the parts of a bulb by cutting a paperwhite or narcissus bulb in half lengthwise. Let your children look at the inside of the bulb and its many parts.

Flowers

Flower Counting Books

For each child, make a six-page booklet with a construction paper cover. On the cover of each book, write "My Flower Counting Book by" and a child's name. Then write a numeral on each page starting with 1 and ending with 5. Give each child 15 flower stickers and have him or her put the number of stickers that corresponds with the numeral written on each page. Have the children complete their books by using a green crayon to add stems and leaves to each of their flower stickers.

Flower Collage

Ask friends and parents to help you collect bulb catalogs. On the floor, place a long sheet of butcher paper, some scissors, the catalogs, and some glue. Let your children cut or tear out pictures of flowers that grow from bulbs. Then have them paste their pictures on the paper, creating a large flower collage to hang on the wall.

Let's Plant Some Bulbs

Sung to: "The Farmer in the Dell"

Let's plant some bulbs,
Let's plant some bulbs,
Hi, ho, down below,
Let's plant some bulbs.

Let's water our bulbs,
Let's water our bulbs,
Hi, ho, water and hoe,
Let's water our bulbs.

Let's watch them grow,
Let's watch them grow,
Hi, ho, watch them go,
Let's watch them grow.

See the pretty flowers,
See the pretty flowers,
Hi, ho, what a show,
See the pretty flowers.

Have children act out planting, watering, and admiring the flowers as they sing.

Jean Warren

Flower Snacks

Set out sliced fruit such as apples, peaches, kiwi, bananas, pitted cherries, and grapes. (Cut cherries and grapes in half to help prevent choking.) On paper plates, let your children arrange the fruit slices in flower shapes.

Did You Ever See a Flower?
Sung to: "Did You Ever See a Lassie?"

Did you ever see a flower, a flower, a flower?
Did you ever see a flower so pretty and tall?
It's swaying and blowing,
In the wind, it is growing.
Did you ever see a flower so pretty and tall?

Have your children pretend to be flowers, growing tall and swaying in the wind.

Beverly Qualheim

Pick a Flower

Collect a variety of plastic and silk flowers, or cut simple flower shapes out of felt. Place the flowers all around the room. Give each child a basket. Let your children walk around the room "picking" the flowers and putting them in their baskets. Sing the song below as the children pick the flowers.

Sung to: "The Paw, Paw Patch"

Pickin' up flowers and puttin' 'em in our baskets,
Pickin' up flowers and puttin' 'em in our baskets,
Pickin' up flowers and puttin' 'em in our baskets,
Way down yonder in our flower patch.

Adapted Traditional

Cup Terrarium

Let your children create their own natural environment—a terrarium—where the moisture evaporates, condenses, then rains down on living plants.

You Will Need

STARTS
two or three of the following indoor plants (must be small): wandering Jew *(Tradescantia fluminensis)*, spiderwort *(Siderasis fuscata)*, polkadot plant *(Hypoestes sanguinolenta)*, star plant *(Cryptanthus bivittatus)*

SUPPLIES
two 20-ounce clear-plastic cups per child

potting soil

washed gravel

pebbles, bark, or marbles

transparent tape or hot glue gun

water

Soil and Location Select a brightly lit area in which to set the terrariums. This light needs to be the brightest light possible that is not in direct sunlight.

Space Choose small plants and a cup large enough so there's a little room for the plants to grow.

Time Required You and your children can enjoy your terrariums right away.

Planting the Terrarium
Give two cups to each child. Have each child put a layer of gravel—about 1 inch deep—in one of the cups. Add potting soil until the cup is half full. Let your children select one or two small plants. Remove the plants from their original containers. Gently massage the roots before planting, and firm the soil around each plant after planting. Have the children add a few pebbles, pieces of bark, or marbles to decorate their terrariums. Water lightly. Place another clear-plastic cup over each child's planted cup and tape or glue them together.

Try This
Many types of containers can be recycled into terrariums. Some salads, sandwiches, sprouts, cupcakes, etc., are sold in clear-plastic containers that have a snap-off lid or a lid that is hinged to the container. You can use any of these containers for terrariums by following the directions to the left.

Care Set the terrariums in bright light. Encourage your children to watch the terrariums each day and note how they cloud up and then water themselves.

What's Happening? Explain that the water evaporates from the soil and then condenses (or gathers) on the top of the terrariums before it rains down on the plants.

The Dirt on Gardening

DO PLANTS NEED LIGHT?

Try this simple experiment. Make three identical Cup Terrariums, using the same kind of plants. Put one Cup Terrarium in bright light and one in partial shade. Completely cover the third terrarium with a dark-colored towel or a lunch bag. After one week, check each terrarium. Have your children note the differences in the plants. Have them check each week for another month. What conclusions can they draw?

Extra Fun

Try making terrariums that start from seed! To make each terrarium, cut the top half off an empty, 1-liter soft-drink bottle. Keep the cap on the bottle. Set the top of the bottle in an aluminum pie pan. Glue the perimeter of the bottle to the pie pan with a hot glue gun. Let the glue harden. Then have your children take the caps off their terrarium bottles. Have your children use funnels to put soil through the tops of the bottles into the pans. Then have them drop in easy-to-grow plant or flower seeds and use the funnels to put a little more soil directly on top of the seeds. Have your children add small amounts of water to their terrariums and put the caps back on. Place the terrariums in bright light.

What Kids Can Do

Your children can each make their own Cup Terrarium. Encourage them to keep the terrariums in the same place, but have them marked so each child can readily identify his or her terrarium.

The Rain Cycle

The Rain Cycle Song
Sung to: "The Farmer in the Dell"

Rain comes falling down,
Rain comes falling down,
Rain falls down upon the ground.
Rain comes falling down.

Roots soak up the rain,
Roots soak up the rain,
Roots say, "Thanks for the rain today."
Roots soak up the rain.

Plants use rain to grow,
Plants use rain to grow,
Plants grow tall when rain does fall.
Plants use rain to grow.

Leaves let out the rain,
Leaves let out the rain,
Leaves let rain out, there is no doubt.
Leaves let out the rain.

The rain turns into vapor,
The rain turns into vapor,
The vapor goes high, making clouds in the sky.
The rain turns into vapor.

Gayle Bittinger

Learning With Terrariums
Have each child fill a small container with soil and plant a small plant. Have the children water their plants using a small eyedropper and place four craft sticks around the edge of the container. Help them slip a plastic bag over the craft sticks to form a cover.

Have your children observe their small terrariums. Do they notice water collecting? Where did it come from? Tell your children about the water cycle in a terrarium. Plants take up water through their roots and then give off water vapor through their leaves. When the water vapor reaches the top of the terrarium, it cools and turns back into water, which in turn becomes heavy and falls back down on the plant.

Rain Books

Give each child a small, plain book that you have made by stapling together four to six sheets of paper with a construction-paper cover. On the front of each book, write "Rain Helps Things Grow by" and a child's name. Let your children look through magazines or seed catalogs and tear out pictures of things that need rain to help them grow, such as trees, flowers, and other plants. Then have the children glue the pictures in their books. Let your children "read" their books to you by naming the things in the pictures.

Rain Painting

On a rainy day, give each child a paper plate. Let the children sprinkle drops of food coloring or small amounts of powered tempera paint onto their plates. Have them put on raincoats, walk outside, and hold up their paper plates in the rain for about a minute. After they bring their plates inside, talk about the designs created by the rain.

Making Rain

Gather your children in a circle. Tell them that they are going to help you make a rainstorm. Begin by rubbing your hands on your thighs. Ask your children to join you in making light "drizzle" sounds. Then make "rain" sounds by lightly clapping your hands on your thighs, then increasing the pressure and speed of the claps in order to develop the rainstorm. When the rainstorm is in full swing, gradually slow down the rain until the storm has cleared.

Container Garden

You don't need a yard at all to make a Container Garden, just some creativity!

You Will Need

SEEDS OR STARTS

edging plants and trailers: fuchsia (*Fuchsia x hybrida*), lobelia (*Lobelia erinus*), petunia (*Petunia x hybrida*), Swan River daisy (*Brachycome iberidifolia*), sweet alyssum (*Lobularia maritima*), verbena (*Verbena x hybrida*)

mid-height plants: dwarf bedding dahlia (*Dahlia merckii*), pansy (*Viola x wittrockiana*), wax leaf begonia (*Begonia semperflorens cultorum*), tuberous begonia (*Begonia solananthera*), stock (*Matthiola incana*)

tall plants: dwarf sunflower (*Helianthus*), flowering tobacco (*Nicotiana*), geranium (*Pelargonium x hortorum*), poor man's orchid (*Schizanthus pinnatus*), snapdragon (*Antirrhinum*), zinnia (*Zinnia elegans*)

SUPPLIES

one container with a water
   tray per child

potting soil

plant seeds or starts

time-release fertilizer

basic gardening tools

Soil and Location You will need good potting soil, available at a garden center or nursery. Place the containers in the appropriately sunny or shady area, depending on the plants you choose.

Space One of the bonuses of container gardening is that you can use as much or as little space as you have available.

Time Required Plant the containers a few weeks after the last danger of frost in your area has passed. The time it takes for your containers to start flowering will depend on the size and age of the plants you use. Your container should look lush and full within a few weeks. As soon as the weather warms up, the plants will start to flower.

Planting the Containers First, decide whether the containers will be located in the sun or the shade, and select plants appropriate to that area. Fill the containers with potting soil, leaving room for the height of the root balls of the plants. Add the recommended amount of fertilizer to the soil. Place taller plants in the middle of the container. Then select plants of medium height. The last plants you will place are the edging or trailing plants that will spill over the sides of the containers. Fill the gap between the plants with more potting soil, making sure that the soil level is even. Place the containers on trays to capture the water, and water the plants thoroughly.

Care Check the containers every few days to see if they need water. If the weather is very warm (80s and above), check the containers every day and water if necessary. Deadhead faded flowers regularly. Toward the end of

the summer, promote new growth in lobelia and sweet alyssum by trimming them back. An application of liquid fertilizer will keep plants flowering if they are starting to slow down.

For More Fun

Let your children make their own plant containers! For each child, gather an empty tin can. Use a hammer and a large nail to poke four or five drainage holes in the bottom of each can. Use a metal file to file off rough edges, or cover rough edges

with duct tape. Set out the cans along with a variety of decorating materials, such as yarn, fabric scraps, construction paper scraps, rickrack, sequins, glitter glue, buttons, and several bottles of glue. Let your children use the decorative materials any way they choose to decorate their containers. Let the children plant flower seeds in their containers or take them home to give as gifts.

What Kids Can Do

Your children can help with every stage of this project. They can be especially helpful by watering and deadheading when necessary.

The Dirt on Gardening

TRANSPLANTING

Gardeners spend much of their time transplanting plants from containers to beds or other containers, or from one spot to another within the garden. Here is a process you and your children might use when transplanting plants in your group's gardens.

1. Carefully ease the plant out of its container by turning the pot upside down and holding  onto the plant as it comes out. If it does not want to slide out, try gently squeezing or slapping the sides and bottom of the pot.

2. If the root ball is solid or matted, you will need to loosen it up by scoring it with a knife. If you don't loosen the root ball, it will keep growing around and around and never spread out.

3. Dig a hole in the desired spot, place the plant in the hole, and fill the hole with potting soil, making sure the top of the root ball is even with the top level of the soil.

4. Make a 2-inch moat shape around the stem of the plant. This will help the soil hold water.

5. Water the transplanted plant thoroughly and fertilize when necessary.

Containers

Sorting Containers

By Type—Set a large variety of containers outside. Encourage your children to sort the containers by type by placing all the baskets in one pile, all the plastic tubs in another pile, etc.

By Size—The next day, ask your children to sort the containers by size by placing the baskets in a line according to size, smallest to largest or largest to smallest.

By Color—Another time, mix up the containers and have your children place them in groups according to color.

Decorating Containers

Give each child a small plant container and a variety of ribbons, rickrack, glue, artificial flowers, old puzzle pieces, buttons, etc. Let your children decorate the containers to give as gifts.

Container Talk

At circle time, set a container in the middle of the circle. Go around the circle and see if your children can think of something they can use the container for. Accept all answers. (Examples: store crayons, put treasures in, take to the beach) If the first version of this game is too hard, help your children out by talking about a place, such as "How could we use this container in the kitchen (in the bathroom, on the porch, at the beach, etc.)?"

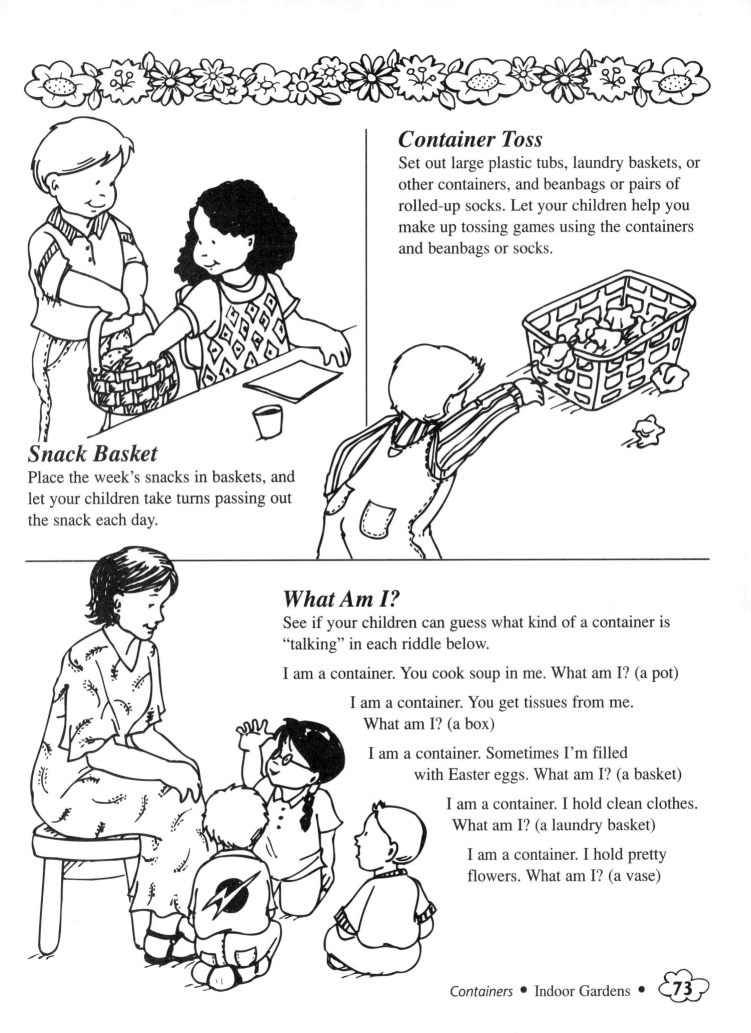

Container Toss

Set out large plastic tubs, laundry baskets, or other containers, and beanbags or pairs of rolled-up socks. Let your children help you make up tossing games using the containers and beanbags or socks.

Snack Basket

Place the week's snacks in baskets, and let your children take turns passing out the snack each day.

What Am I?

See if your children can guess what kind of a container is "talking" in each riddle below.

I am a container. You cook soup in me. What am I? (a pot)

I am a container. You get tissues from me. What am I? (a box)

I am a container. Sometimes I'm filled with Easter eggs. What am I? (a basket)

I am a container. I hold clean clothes. What am I? (a laundry basket)

I am a container. I hold pretty flowers. What am I? (a vase)

Indoor Garden

Green things can grow any time of the year. When the weather outside is cold, let your children bring summer indoors with these unique gardens.

You Will Need

basic gardening tools

FOR CARROT GARDEN

three large carrots without stems

plastic bowl or other shallow container

knife

pebbles

water

FOR SWEET POTATO GARDEN

sweet potato with little purple bumps or a few thin, white roots

toothpicks

clear jar

water

Carrot Garden

Location Two indoor counters or shelves—one that receives bright, indirect light, one that receives direct sunlight.

Space Just enough room for your containers.

Time Required Leaves should begin to appear within a week. Each carrot top can support leaves for only about three weeks.

Tip

Make and display a watering chart to remind children to check the water levels every few days for each of these Indoor Gardens.

What to Do Have your children select three large carrots and pluck off any old leaves. Cut 2 inches off each carrot. (Save the remaining carrot pieces to use for snacks.) Have your children place each carrot, cut-side-down, in a bowl or other shallow container, and place pebbles around the carrots to hold each one in place. Have the children add enough water to cover the carrots halfway. Place the carrot-filled bowl in a place that gets plenty of indirect sunlight.

Care Keep the water level in the container at the same level.

What to Expect Within a week, small green leaves will start growing from the carrot tops. When the leaves appear, place the container in direct sunlight.

Variation Try this with other root vegetables, such as beets and radishes. For these, use the entire vegetable instead of cutting off the top 2 inches.

Sweet Potato Garden

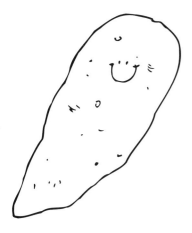

Location Two indoor counters or shelves—one that is warm and shady; one that receives bright light.

Space Just enough room for your containers.

Time Required Several weeks. The sweet potato will provide enough food to support the viny leaves for a couple of months.

What to Do Find a sweet potato that has little purple bumps on its skin or one that has grown a few thin, white roots. Place the narrow end of the potato in a jar. Hold the potato in the jar by sticking three or four toothpicks around the middle of the potato. Add warm water to the jar until the potato is covered halfway. Place the jar in a warm, shady place. Change the water weekly, always using warm water.

What to Expect In about two weeks, white roots will grow from the bottom of the sweet potato, and later, stems. Place the potato in a bright area, and leaves will soon grow.

What Kids Can Do

Except for cutting off the tops of the carrots, young children can help with every stage of these Indoor Gardens.

The Dirt on Gardening

PROPAGATION

Plants can grow from seeds, bulbs, or cuttings. Depending on the type of plant, cuttings can be started either in water, directly in soil, or by first dipping the end in a rooting compound and then placing it in potting soil. Consult a local nursery or cooperative extension service about specific plants and methods.

If your children grew sweet potato vines, they have the perfect source for a lesson about propagation.

When the vinelike stems with leaves grow long enough, help your children cut off several pieces of vine, each about 6 inches long. Place the ends of the cuttings in a small, clear container of water. Let your children check the container each day and add water as needed. Soon they will see roots, and later, more vines will grow. The sweet potato has propagated in water from just a 6-inch cutting!

Impatiens provide the perfect source for propagating in soil with a rooting compound (available at garden centers). Take 3- to 4-inch cuttings, and make a clean cut just below one of the leaf nodes (where the leaf stalk joins the stem). Remove all but two or three pairs of leaves at the top of the cutting. Dip the cut end into rooting compound, and push each cutting gently into a sandy compost. Water lightly, then enclose in a plastic "tent" (clear plastic bags with ties work well). Avoid direct sunlight. Allow several weeks for roots to form.

Indoor Garden Fun

Seed Viewing Jar

Use a pint jar and three paper towels. Fill the jar with water to saturate the paper towels. Pour out all but 1 inch of water. Place two dried mung beans between the paper towels and the jar, 1 inch apart. The paper towels should cling to the inside of the jar. To make sure that the paper towel remains firmly against the glass, stuff crumpled wet paper towels into the center of the jar. Monitor the water level daily to make sure it doesn't go below 1 inch. Place the jar in a warm, dark place. This method makes for great viewing as the bean seeds begin to sprout.

Mold Garden

This activity may sound awful, but it is actually quite fascinating to young children. To make this "garden," sprinkle a piece of bread with a teaspoon of water and put the bread into a clear plastic bag. Blow air into the bag, and close it securely with a twist tie. Place the bag in a warm, dark place. After five or six days, little mold spots will begin appearing on the bread. Keep the bag closed, and let your children observe as the mold continues to grow. At the end of the project, throw out the unopened bag.

Grass and Alfalfa Seed Friends

Mr. Potato Head—Gather a potato for each child. Cut ½ inch or so off both ends of each potato. Stand the potatoes upright on a flat surface, and use a melon-baller to scoop out holes in the top ends. Have your children place two cotton balls in their potato's scooped-out top. Let the children sprinkle some water on the cotton balls and then sprinkle on grass seeds. Carve out a face on one side of each of the potatoes, and place them in a sunny spot. Watch the grassy "hair" grow.

Cup Faces—Have your children decorate paper cups to resemble faces. Fill the cups with dirt. Let your children sprinkle grass seeds on top of the dirt and add water. Place the cups in a sunny area, and soon the Cup Faces will grow hair.

Sprout Pets—For each child, trace an animal shape on a sponge and cut it out (tracing around cookie cutters makes this easy). Place each shape in a shallow container such as a clean, frozen-food tray. Pour on enough water so that the sponges are completely saturated and there is water pooling in the containers. Help your children sprinkle alfalfa seeds on their shapes. Place the shapes in a warm area, and in a few days, your children's "pets" will begin to sprout alfalfa "hair."

Variation: A week or more before St. Patrick's Day, have your children sprinkle grass seeds onto a sponge cut in the shape of a shamrock. They'll have grassy shamrocks in time for the holiday.

Gardening With Pits

Help your children collect avocado pits. Carefully poke toothpicks into the pits, and let your children set them on the rim of a large glass or jar. Fill the glasses with water so that the bottom halves of the pits are under water. Each day, let your children add more water to keep the level constant. Help your children keep a record of their plants' growth.

Tent Garden

Your children will love playing in this living tent! Use annuals to plant a tent for summer use, or plant a year-round tent with evergreen vines.

You Will Need

SEEDS OR STARTS

annuals: cardinal climber (*Ipomoea x multifida*), love-in-a-puff (*Cardiospermum halicacabum*), morning glory (*Ipomoea*), moonflower (*Ipomoea alba*), trailing variety nasturtium (*Tropaeolum majus*), runner bean (*Phaseolus coccineus*), sweet pea (*Lathyurs odoratus*), sweet potato vine (*Ipomoea batatas "Blackie"*), trumpet vine (*Campsis radicans*)

evergreens: evergreen armandi clematis (*Dlematis armandii*), honeysuckle (*Lonicera x brownii "Dropmore Scarlet"*), winter-creeper (*Euonymus fortunei var. radicans "Variegatus"*), winter jasmine (*Jasminum nudiflorum*)

SUPPLIES

six 6-foot-tall bamboo poles

two sticks or stakes

string

round piece of cardboard or plastic

netting (optional)

Soil and Location Your Tent Garden will need at least six hours of full sun, and average, well-drained soil.

Space At least a 5-foot-by-5-foot area.

Time Required It will take four to six weeks for the plants to start forming a dense enough cover to resemble a tent.

Planting the Garden After choosing the right spot, prepare the soil as you normally would for any other new garden. Determine where the center of the tent will be and draw an X in the dirt. Cut a length of string that is the length of half of the diameter the tent will be, plus 3 inches (for tying). Tie the string to the middle of a stake. Insert the stake into the middle of the X until the string is about 3 inches from the ground. Tie a short stake to the end of the string, pull it taut, and draw a circle all the way around the stake in the center. (See the illustration below.)

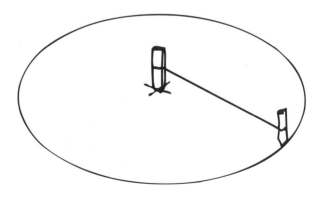

Gather six 6-foot-tall bamboo poles. Begin placing the poles around the circle, leaving enough room between two of the poles so that your children can crawl through to enter the tent. Position the poles firmly in the soil, and tie the poles together at the top with string. If desired, surround the poles with netting to make climbing easier for the plants.

A few weeks after all danger of frost has passed, evenly sow the seeds or plant the starts around the tent structure. To prevent weeds from growing, place plastic or cardboard on the floor inside the tent.

Care You will need to help guide new seedlings up the poles, water, and deadhead your garden.

What Kids Can Do

Your children can help plant the seeds or starts around the tent structure, water, and help guide the plants up the poles. Children can also help harvest runner bean pods for eating or for planting next year. And of course, the children can enjoy their living tent!

Rain Gauge

To measure the amount of water you are giving your garden, make a rain gauge. Find a clean, straight-sided container, such as a coffee can or a glass jar. Use a permanent marker and a ruler to measure and mark every quarter-inch on the outside of the can, starting at the bottom. Find an unsheltered spot in the garden that receives an average amount of rainfall and water from your sprinkler. Make sure nothing hangs over the mouth of the jar. Secure your gauge by pushing it into the ground a half inch or so. After each rain or watering, measure the amount of water in the can and record it in your garden journal. The water level should average an inch a week.

The Dirt on Gardening

WATER CONSERVATION

An average garden needs about 1 inch of rainfall each week. How often your garden needs water is determined by the following factors:

- Type of plants—each type grows at a different rate
- Type of soil—sandy soil will dry out more quickly than clay
- Exposure to wind
- Depth and type of mulch
- Amount of rainfall
- Amount of organic matter you add to your soil

To conserve water in your garden, try putting up a short fence to block the wind. This will reduce the amount of evaporation from the leaves of your plants. Make sure your fence isn't so high that it blocks sunlight from your garden.

Good mulching will also decrease the amount of water that you need to use in your garden.

Encourage roots to grow stronger and deeper by watering thoroughly instead of just giving the garden a sprinkle.

There are many benefits to watering your garden early in the morning or late in the evening: less water will evaporate in the sun, your plants will dry off properly without getting moldy or rotting, and the roots will store more water so they can spend the rest of the day growing and resting.

Tents

Classroom Tent

Bring in a small self-standing pup tent. Place it in the book corner to encourage quiet book reading, or in the block area to encourage camp play. Wherever you put it, your children will find a use for it. You may want to discuss with your children what your tent could be. Each week, turn it into something different. Ideas include a house, a hospital, a bear cave, an igloo, a bird's nest, etc.

Variations: If you don't have access to a tent, there are other structures that work just as well. Try draping blankets over a card table or a large furniture box. You might try asking parents to help build your group a child-size teepee.

Texture Tents

Cut tent shapes out of several different types of paper, such as glossy paper, handmade paper, corrugated cardboard, sandpaper, newsprint, etc. At circle time, pass out the tent shapes, and have your children describe how they feel. Then play a matching game with them. Hand each child a tent shape. Choose one child to hold up a tent and then walk around until he or she finds a match. Continue until everyone is matched up. Later, place the tent shapes in a box, and keep them with your table toys. Encourage your children to sort them by matching up pairs.

I Like to Play in a Tent

Sung to: "The Farmer in the Dell"

I like to play in a tent,
I like to play in a tent.
Heigh, ho, away I go.
I like to play in a tent.

Sometimes my tent is a house,
Sometimes my tent is a house.
Heigh, ho, away I go.
Sometimes my tent is a house.

Additional verses: Sometimes my tent is a garage, a hospital, a bank, a store, a bedroom, etc.

Jean Warren

Tent Snack

Serve your children snacks in their tent. Give four children at a time their snack, and be sure the tent is cleaned up before the next group has its snack. Suggested snacks include apple sections, cheese and crackers, trail mix, orange sections, dried fruit, etc. For this activity, drinks would probably be best served outside of the tent.

Group Mural

Set out triangle rubber stamps and stamp pads. Tape a long piece of butcher paper to a table. Have your children make a tent mural by using the triangle stamps to stamp "tent" shapes all over the paper. Later, hang your group mural low on a wall for everyone to enjoy.

Seed Garden

Many plants produce interesting seed heads that are easily identifiable. Your children will have fun learning how plants reproduce themselves!

You Will Need

SEEDS OR STARTS
love-in-a-puff (*Cardiospermum halicacabum*), love-in-a-mist (*Nigella damascena*), lupine (*Lupinus*), pumpkin, scarlet runner beans (*Phaseolus coccineus*), spider plant (*Cleome hasslerana*), sunflower (*Helianthus annuus*), poppies (*Papaver somniferum*)

SUPPLIES
basic gardening tools

Soil and Location These plants need a minimum of six hours of sunlight and fertile, well-drained soil.

Space Your Seed Garden should have an area that is about 4-foot-by-8-foot. The pumpkins need the extra length to sprawl out.

Time Required The seed heads will mature in three or four months.

Planting the Garden Choose seeds or starts from the list. Lupine, a perennial that blooms in the spring, can be started from seeds planted in the winter or early spring. The rest of the plants can be started from seed when weather in your area is warm. Plant the taller plants, such as the spider plants and the sunflowers, in the back of the garden. Use the sunflowers as a living support for the runner beans and love-in-a-puff, which are vines. Plant the shorter plants, such as poppies, lupine, and love-in-a-mist, in front. The pumpkins can sprawl around the entire outer edge of the Seed Garden, providing a living mulch.

What Kids Can Do

Your children can help plant, water, harvest the seed heads, and scoop out the pumpkin seeds.

Care You will need to water and weed your Seed Garden. You and your children can enjoy all of the beauty of this garden until the plants go to seed. For seed collecting procedures, see "The Dirt on Gardening" section to the right.

Did You Know?

Some plants re-seed themselves! Some annuals such as cosmos, lobelia, sweet alyssum, and sunflowers will re-seed themselves if you let them bloom, die, and drop their seeds to the ground. Most perennials, such as chives, foxglove, and lamb's-ear, do this all by themselves.

Some plants, such as roses and beans, produce a seed pod. The seeds complete their growing inside a hard shell that provides it with enough stored energy to mature completely. Some seed pods are so hard that a bird or animal has to break them open before the seeds can be released. Of course, some seeds become the bird's or animal's dinner, but there are usually enough seeds inside the pod to ensure that a portion will make its way to the ground. If you have plants that form seed pods, let the pods dry completely, break them open, and collect and store the seeds like you would any other type of seeds.

The Dirt on Gardening

COLLECTING SEEDS

Once your blooms have shriveled and started to dry out, remove the whole flower head. Use the method described below to dry the heads immediately so they do not get moldy.

Store the seed heads and pods in shallow boxes. Lay them out in a thin layer with space between them. Let the blooms dry out completely for a week or two. Then gently break them open over a clean sheet of paper that has been folded in half and then unfolded. Use the paper as a makeshift funnel to help pour the seeds into a small envelope labeled with the type of flower, the year it was saved, and the color of the bloom. Put the envelopes in airtight containers such as Mason jars or resealable freezer bags. Add an envelope of silica gel (available at garden centers) to each jar or bag to keep the seeds dry. Store your jars or bags in a cool, dry place. Don't be surprised if the plants that emerge from collected seeds aren't exactly like the plant they were harvested from. Some seeds may revert back to the original species from which they were bred.

Seeds

Seed Pictures

Seed Plates—Give each of your children a paper plate and a pile of dried seeds such as pumpkin seeds, popcorn, sunflower seeds, or sesame seeds. Show your children how to glue the seeds in an interesting design on the plates.

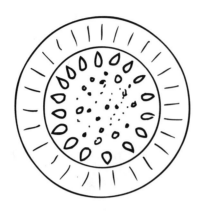

Dough Seed Pictures—Give your children margarine tub lids and a lump of modeling dough. Have the children flatten the modeling dough into their lids and then use the seeds to make designs in the dough.

Sunflower Pictures—Give each child a small yellow paper plate and eight strips of yellow tissue paper. Have the children glue the strips around the edges of the paper plate. Then have them glue sunflower seeds in the middle of the plate. When the glue dries, attach construction-paper stems to each sunflower and display them around your room.

Seeds for Snacks

Give each of your children a small, resealable plastic bag. Set out bowls of different seed snacks such as pumpkin seeds or sunflower seeds. Have your children spoon some seeds into their bags and then enjoy them for a snack.

Seed Display

While studying different kinds of seeds, encourage your children to bring in seeds from home. These could be from fruits, vegetables, flowers, or nuts. As the seeds are brought in, put identical seeds together in small, resealable plastic bags. To the top of each bag, staple a label with the name of the seeds and a picture of where the seeds have come from. Hang the bags on a bulletin board to make a seed display, or put them all together in an album-type book for your children to study in their free time.

Seed Estimation

Place 10 to 20 seeds in a baby food jar. Let your children guess how many seeds there are. After everyone has had a turn guessing, take the seeds out and count them with your children. Were their guesses close?

Seed Transporting

Ask each child's parents to send in a large pair of old white socks. Have your children slip the socks on over their shoes. Take the children on a seed-collecting walk. If possible, walk through a park, a meadow, a field, or some woods. As you walk along, have your children look at their socks every now and then. Do they see any seeds? Where did the seeds come from? What will happen when they shake the seeds off their socks when they get back? Explain to them that this is the way seeds get moved, or transported, to new areas when they fall to the ground. What are other ways that seeds might get transported?

Extension: Have the children carefully shake some of their seeds onto a tray of soil. Place the tray in a sunny place and add water regularly. What happens?

Seed Dramatics

Explain how plants grow, then have your children act out the poem below.

Dig, dig, dig,
> (Pretend to dig.)
Rake just so,
> (Pretend to rake.)
Plant the seeds.
> (Bend over and plant seeds.)
Watch them grow.
> (Put hands on hips.)

Tug, tug, tug,
Pull up weeds.
> (Pretend to pull weeds.)
Sun and rain,
> (Put hands up to make sun and have them falling down to make rain.)
My garden needs.

Up, up, up,
> (Squat down.)
Green stems climb.
> (Stand up slowly.)
Open wide—
> (Spread out arms to form circle over heads.)
It's blossom time.
> (Big smiles.)

Jean Warren

Rock Garden

Your children will be amazed to see plants and flowers grow out of rocks!

You Will Need

STARTS

ground covers: sea pinks (*Armeria maritima*), snow-in-summer (*Cerastium tomentosum*), stonecrop (*Sedum*), coralbells (*Heuchera sanguinea*), blue fescue (*Festuca ovina glauca*), creeping thyme (*Thymus serpyllum*), wooly thyme (*Thymus psuedolanuginosus*), carpathian bell flower (*Campanula carpatica*)

perennials: cottage pinks (*Dianthus plumarius*), rock rose (*Cistus hybridus*), rosemary (*Rosmarinus officinalis*), beard-tongue (*Penstemon pinifollius*)

bulbs: crocus, snowdrop

SUPPLIES

basic gardening tools

rocks of various sizes

potting soil

compost or other organic matter

Soil and Location A great place to start is in an area that already contains rocks. Or, choose a spot that naturally slopes. If you don't have such an area available, bring in topsoil and compost and make your own slope, also known as a "berm."

Space Your Rock Garden will need a 5-foot-by-3-foot space.

Time Required It will take an hour or two to create a berm, and a few more hours to place the rocks and plants.

Planting the Garden Make sure you have a variety of sizes of rocks. The more irregular the shape of the rocks, the better. If you can get it, limestone is a good choice. It is porous, allowing moisture to seep through, and some roots may even be able to grow into the limestone.

Tip

If you would like to try growing plants in small, hard-to-reach areas, try putting some seeds onto a piece of paper that has been folded in half. Place the paper into narrow crevasses and simply blow the seeds in.

When placing the rocks, start from the bottom of the berm and work your way up. Bury at least one quarter to one half of the bottom row of rocks in the soil. As you place the rocks, make sure you leave spaces here and there for plants. After you finish placing the rocks, fill in spaces with soil. Let the soil settle for a few days before you add plants.

To plant your Rock Garden, place starts or bulbs in crevasses, tamping the soil around them thoroughly and adding soil if necessary. Water each of your starts after planting.

Care You will need to regularly weed and deadhead spent flowers. Occasionally, trim back leggy plants and divide any plant that has become too big for its space.

The Dirt on Gardening

STEPPING STONES

Every garden could use a few stepping stones to help define a pathway, or to be used as garden art. Stepping stone kits are available at craft stores, or you can make your stones from scratch. To make group stepping stones, collect the following materials: molds, which can be plastic flowerpot saucers, aluminum pie pans, or small plastic garbage can lids; four pounds of finishing concrete mix, such as Quickrete, for each stone; and decorative items such as marbles, pebbles, colored sea-glass, or seashells.

Prepare the concrete mix, and spray the molds very lightly with vegetable cooking spray. Fill the molds to within ⅛ inch of the tops. Set out the decorative materials, and gather your children together. Encourage your children to lightly press the items of their choice into the concrete. Let the stones dry for at least 24 hours. When the concrete is dry, turn the molds over, and gently pull back on the edges of each mold. The stones should come easily out of the molds. Let your children choose where in your garden to place the stones.

Rocks

Rock Family Stories

Have each child go to the discovery table and choose three to five rocks. Tell the children that the rocks are a rock family. Ask the children to tell you a short story about his or her rock family. Write down each child's story, and then let him or her draw pictures of the rock family to go with his or her story.

Rock Hunt

Ask your children where they would look for rocks to collect. Where are rocks found? Then take your children on a walk to collect rocks. Encourage them to look for rocks of various shapes and sizes. Bring the rocks back to your room, and display them on a discovery table.

Rock Sorting

Encourage your children to sort the rocks on your discovery table according to size or shape or another classification the children think of. Discuss how rocks are alike and how they are different.

I Love Rocks
Sung to: "Three Blind Mice"

I love rocks,
I love rocks.
In a garden,
In a box.

I love to see them in the street.
I love to feel them under my feet.
I love to hold them, what a treat!

I love rocks,
I love rocks.

Jean Warren

Rock Examination
Set out various types of rocks, including a container of gravel and some magnifying glasses. Let your children take turns looking at the different rocks through a magnifying glass. What do they see? Have the children smell the rocks. What do the rocks smell like? How do the rocks feel? Are they rough or smooth?

Pebble Pictures
Set out a variety of pebbles, glue, and squares of cardboard. Let your children glue the pebbles to the cardboard squares to create Pebble Pictures.

Mr. McGregor's Garden

Before Mrs. Rabbit went out one morning, she warned her four bunnies—Flopsy, Mopsy, Cotton-tail, and Peter—not to go into Mr. McGregor's garden. But that's exactly where Peter ran straight away. You and your children can begin a delightful storytelling adventure with this fun, but long-term, garden project.

You Will Need

SEEDS OR STARTS
any number of the following:
- lettuce (any variety)
- beans (bush or pole)
- radishes
- parsley
- cucumbers
- cabbage
- potatoes
- onions
- chamomile
- gooseberries

SUPPLIES
basic gardening tools

statuary, cutout characters, or props that tell the story

The Tale of Peter Rabbit by Beatrix Potter

Soil and Location Fertile, well-drained soil in full sun.

Space Allow enough room to add garden art or to get as elaborate (with a small garden shed or rabbit's den) as time and your children's imaginations permit.

Time Required For direct seeding, anticipate approximately 70 to 120 days. With starts, allow approximately 40 to 80 days.

Planting the Garden Plan how you want your garden to tell the story of Peter Rabbit in Mr. McGregor's garden, and put your thoughts on paper. Consider putting chamomile near the rabbit den (Mother Rabbit made Peter chamomile tea). Try to put the vegetables that you select in the order that they appear in the story—lettuces, beans, and radishes—where Peter would enter the garden. Parsley could be planted in a corner for Peter to search for to soothe his sick tummy. Peter first encounters McGregor planting cabbages near the cucumbers. Later, he loses one shoe among the cabbages and the other one among the potatoes. Place gooseberries and supporting netting where Peter becomes tangled, and onions near the gate where Peter makes his escape.

Follow directions on seed packages for direct sowing or carefully transplant starts in marked areas.

What Kids Can Do
Your children can help with many parts of this garden! They can help mark the rows, plant the seeds, water, and weed. They will especially enjoy setting props in place, but caution children not to step on young plants in the process.

Care With seeds, thin according to package directions when the seedlings reach the recommended height. For both seeds and starts, weed and water as needed. Support beans and berries with proper trellising.

Harvesting You'll probably want to enjoy your garden before you harvest much from it. The radishes will ripen quickly. They can be left in the ground to help tell the story but will not be good to eat if they get too large. Cucumbers, beans, parsley, and berries can be harvested easily without ruining the display. You can gradually thin and use lettuce, cabbage, and onions, while still preserving the look of your garden.

The Dirt on Gardening

TOOL CARE

Garden work is easiest when the right tool is used for a job and when that tool is kept clean, in good repair, and within easy reach.

To prevent the spread of plant diseases, scrape the dirt off all tools after each use and rinse with water. An old nylon dish scrubber works well. Store all tools in a dry place. Hand trowels keep best in a bucket of sand. At the end of gardening season, thoroughly clean your tools, wipe them with a little oil (or spray them with WD40), and put them back in storage.

Extra Fun

Find or make garden statuary of Mr. McGregor and Peter Rabbit and add them to your garden. Actual statues of the characters can be found at some nurseries and through mail-order catalogs. Depending on your skills or the help you have available, you can make the characters yourself. Cut the character shapes out of wood, paint them, and mount them on stakes. You could even draw and color the characters on posterboard, cover them with self-stick paper, and then mount them in the garden.

If you wish, you can do without actual characters by simply adding props from the story. A hoe and watering can will bring Mr. McGregor's presence to the garden. For Peter, hang a small blue jacket in a scarecrowlike manner, and dangle shoes below the jacket. Turn one corner of the garden into the rabbits' home with a small basket for picking blackberries and a tea kettle for the chamomile tea Mother Rabbit made for Peter before putting him to bed.

Telling the Story

When your garden begins maturing, turn it into a story corner. Gather your children around the garden and read them *The Tale of Peter Rabbit*. As you share the story, point to props or characters in your garden to make the story come alive. Close your storytime with bread, milk, blackberries, and chamomile tea.

Bunnies

Bunny Hop-Along

Let one child begin by rolling a large die
and calling out the number that comes up.
Then have everyone hop that many times.
Let each child have a turn rolling the die.

Counting Carrots

Take your children out to your garden and let
them take turns pulling up and counting carrots.
If your carrots aren't ready for harvesting, fill a
plastic dishpan with dirt. "Plant" ten real carrots
in the dirt. Let each child have a turn pulling up
the carrots and counting them.

Fluffy Bunnies

Give each child a construction-paper
bunny shape. Have your children pull
cotton pillow stuffing or cotton balls
into soft, fluffy pieces and glue them
all over their bunny shapes. From pink
construction paper, cut out ear shapes
that are slightly smaller than the ears
on the bunnies, and cut circles for eyes
out of blue construction paper. Then let
your children glue the ears and eyes
onto their cotton bunnies.

Flannelboard Bunnies

Cut five bunny shapes out of felt and decorate them as the poem below indicates. Place the appropriate bunnies on a flannelboard as you recite the poem below.

This little bunny has two pink eyes.
This little bunny is very wise.
This little bunny is soft as silk.
This little bunny is white as milk.
This little bunny nibbles away
At cabbages and carrots
All the livelong day!

Author Unknown

Bunny Tea Party

At snacktime, set up a tea party for your children and their stuffed bunnies. Serve carrots and lettuce and tea, of course!

Bunny Predictions

Let your children bring in stuffed bunnies from home. Ask them to show each other their bunnies and to predict which bunny is the shortest, which is the tallest, and which bunnies have the longest and the shortest ears. Compare the predictions with the actual answers.

Glossary

annual   a plant that lives for one year or season

bud   a small, compact growth that develops into a leaf, flower, or branch

bulb   a compact package containing a bud, roots, and stored food

compost   decayed organic material, used to improve the quality of soil

deadhead   snipping or pinching faded flowers; promotes new blossoms

dividing   digging up a plant and dividing it into sections to make new plants

drainage   the movement of water through the soil near a plant's root area; "Good drainage" means water drains quickly through the soil. "Bad drainage" means the water drains slowly through the soil.

germinate   the first sprout or growth of a seed

harden off   slowly exposing a plant that has been grown under shelter (indoors or in a greenhouse) to the outdoor environment

maturation   a plant that has reached its flowering stage (includes fruits and vegetables)

mulch   organic material that is placed on top of soil; Mulch conserves moisture in the soil.

organic matter   material of organic origin; Leaves, moss, compost, and manure are all organic matter.

perennial   a plant that lives for more than one season

pesticide   chemical treatments that kill bugs that are harmful to gardens

rooting compound   a hormone powder that enhances the growth of roots on plant cuttings

seedling   a seed that has recently sprouted and grown roots

sow   planting seeds directly in soil indoors or outdoors

starts   plants that have been grown in containers in preparation for replanting outdoors or indoors

thinning   removing seedlings so that remaining plants have the room they need to continue growing

till   mixing compost or other organic material into the soil; This can be done by hand or by using garden tools such as spades or hoes.

T♦tline
PUBLICATIONS

Teacher Resources

ART SERIES
Ideas for successful art experiences.
Cooperative Art
Special Day Art
Outdoor Art

BEST OF TOTLINE® SERIES
Totline's best ideas.
Best of Totline Newsletter
Best of Totline Bear Hugs
Best of Totline Parent Flyers

BUSY BEES SERIES
Seasonal ideas for twos and threes.
Fall • Winter • Spring • Summer

CELEBRATIONS SERIES
Early learning through celebrations.
Small World Celebrations
Special Day Celebrations
Great Big Holiday Celebrations
Celebrating Likes and Differences

CIRCLE TIME SERIES
Put the spotlight on circle time!
Introducing Concepts at Circle Time
Music and Dramatics at Circle Time
Storytime Ideas for Circle Time

EMPOWERING KIDS SERIES
Positive solutions to behavior issues.
Can-Do Kids
Problem-Solving Kids

EXPLORING SERIES
Versatile, hands-on learning.
Exploring Sand • Exploring Water

FOUR SEASONS
Active learning through the year.
Art • Math • Movement • Science

JUST RIGHT PATTERNS
8-page, reproducible pattern folders.
Valentine's Day • St. Patrick's Day •
Easter • Halloween • Thanksgiving •
Hanukkah • Christmas • Kwanzaa •
Spring • Summer • Autumn •
Winter • Air Transportation • Land
Transportation • Service Vehicles
• Water Transportation • Train
• Desert Life • Farm Life • Forest
Life • Ocean Life • Wetland Life
• Zoo Life • Prehistoric Life

KINDERSTATION SERIES
Learning centers for kindergarten.
Calculation Station
Communication Station
Creation Station
Investigation Station

1•2•3 SERIES
Open-ended learning.
Art • Blocks • Games • Colors •
Puppets • Reading & Writing •
Math • Science • Shapes

1001 SERIES
Super reference books.
1001 Teaching Props
1001 Teaching Tips
1001 Rhymes & Fingerplays

PIGGYBACK® SONG BOOKS
New lyrics sung to favorite tunes!
Piggyback Songs
More Piggyback Songs
Piggyback Songs for Infants
and Toddlers
Holiday Piggyback Songs
Animal Piggyback Songs
Piggyback Songs for School
Piggyback Songs to Sign
Spanish Piggyback Songs
More Piggyback Songs for School

PROJECT BOOK SERIES
*Reproducible, cross-curricular project
books and project ideas.*
Start With Art
Start With Science

REPRODUCIBLE RHYMES
*Make-and-take-home books for
emergent readers.*
Alphabet Rhymes • Object Rhymes

SNACKS SERIES
Nutrition combines with learning.
Super Snacks • Healthy Snacks •
Teaching Snacks • Multicultural Snacks

TERRIFIC TIPS
Handy resources with valuable ideas.
Terrific Tips for Directors
Terrific Tips for Toddler Teachers
Terrific Tips for Preschool Teachers

THEME-A-SAURUS® SERIES
Classroom-tested, instant themes.
Theme-A-Saurus
Theme-A-Saurus II
Toddler Theme-A-Saurus
Alphabet Theme-A-Saurus
Nursery Rhyme Theme-A-Saurus
Storytime Theme-A-Saurus
Multisensory Theme-A-Saurus
Transportation Theme-A-Saurus
Field Trip Theme-A-Saurus

TODDLER RESOURCES
Great for working with 18 mos–3 yrs.
Playtime Props for Toddlers
Toddler Art

Parent Resources

A YEAR OF FUN SERIES
Age-specific books for parenting.
Just for Babies • Just for Ones •
Just for Twos • Just for Threes •
Just for Fours • Just for Fives

LEARN WITH PIGGYBACK® SONGS
*Captivating music with
age-appropriate themes.*
Songs & Games for…
Babies • Toddlers • Threes • Fours
Sing a Song of…
Letters • Animals • Colors • Holidays
• Me • Nature • Numbers

LEARN WITH STICKERS
*Beginning workbook and first reader
with 100-plus stickers.*
Balloons • Birds • Bows • Bugs •
Butterflies • Buttons • Eggs • Flags •
Flowers • Hearts • Leaves • Mittens

MY FIRST COLORING BOOK
*White illustrations on black back-
grounds—perfect for toddlers!*
All About Colors
All About Numbers
Under the Sea
Over and Under
Party Animals
Tops and Bottoms

PLAY AND LEARN
Activities for learning through play.
Blocks • Instruments • Kitchen
Gadgets • Paper • Puppets • Puzzles

RAINY DAY FUN
*This activity book for parent-child fun
keeps minds active on rainy days!*

RHYME & REASON STICKER WORKBOOKS
*Sticker fun to boost
language development and
thinking skills.*
Up in Space
All About Weather
At the Zoo
On the Farm
Things That Go
Under the Sea

SEEDS FOR SUCCESS
*Ideas to help children develop
essential life skills for future success.*
Growing Creative Kids
Growing Happy Kids
Growing Responsible Kids
Growing Thinking Kids

THEME CALENDARS
Activities for every day.
Toddler Theme Calendar
Preschool Theme Calendar
Kindergarten Theme Calendar

TIME TO LEARN
Ideas for hands-on learning.
Colors • Letters • Measuring •
Numbers • Science • Shapes •
Matching and Sorting • New Words
• Cutting and Pasting •
Drawing and Writing • Listening •
Taking Care of Myself

Posters
Celebrating Childhood Posters
Reminder Posters

Puppet Pals
Instant puppets!
Children's Favorites • The Three Bears
• Nursery Rhymes • Old MacDonald
• More Nursery Rhymes • Three
Little Pigs • Three Billy Goats Gruff •
Little Red Riding Hood

Manipulatives
CIRCLE PUZZLES
African Adventure Puzzle

LITTLE BUILDER STACKING CARDS
Castle • The Three Little Pigs

Tot-Mobiles
*Each set includes four punch-out,
easy-to-assemble mobiles.*
Animals & Toys
Beginning Concepts
Four Seasons

Start right, start bright!